DISCRIMINATION

CHINESE AMERICANS STRUGGLE FOR EQUALITY

DISCRIMINATION

CHINESE AMERICANS STRUGGLE FOR EQUALITY

by
FRANKLIN NG

Rourke Corporation, Inc.
Vero Beach, Florida 32964

Cover design: David Hundley

Library of Congress Cataloging-in-Publication Data
Ng, Franklin, 1947-
    Chinese Americans struggle for equality / by Franklin
Ng.
        p.   cm. — (Discrimination)
    Includes bibliographical references and index.
    Summary: Identifies discrimination and discusses how
Chinese Americans have struggled for their civil rights.
    ISBN 0-86593-181-X (alk. paper)
    1. Chinese Americans — Civil rights — Juvenile litera-
ture.   [1. Chinese Americans — Civil rights.   2. Ethnic
relations.]   I. Title.   II. Series.
E184.06N42   1992   92-7472
323.1′1951073 — dc20   CIP
                                                          AC

PRINTED IN THE UNITED STATES OF AMERICA

CONTENTS

DISCRIMINATION

CHINESE AMERICANS STRUGGLE FOR EQUALITY

1 What Is Discrimination?

Prejudice and discrimination may be found wherever people make social distinctions. The various groups in a society are ranked according to different statuses, which may be dominant or subordinate, superior or inferior. The differences in caste, class, language, religion, and race or ethnicity may be the basis for social differences or social ranking.

Prejudice can be defined as a negative attitude towards a category of people. Prejudice involves ideas, thoughts, and beliefs. Children can easily acquire prejudice by learning it from their parents and those in their neighborhoods and schools. From those with whom they are in contact, they can pick up values and biases that are critical towards those who are different. They can divide people into categories of a "we-group" or "in-group" versus a "they-group" or "out-group." The culture of the former is judged favorably, while that of the latter is seen as strange, foolish, or deviant.

It is not uncommon to hear children say about their peers: "What a weird group! Their last names sound odd. They have unusual habits. Don't they dress funny? They eat strange foods. They speak with a foreign accent. They practice a superstitious religion." Children often do reflect the concerns of adults, but they can also be very honest and direct about their feelings.

Ethnocentrism

There are many forms of prejudice, but a good place to begin is with the concept of ethnocentrism. Anthropologists who study the diversity of humankind note that all peoples exhibit ethnocentrism. This is the belief that one's own culture, lifestyle, and values are better than those of another group. For most people, it is easy to assume that those behaviors that one is more familiar with are more desirable than those that are strange or different. The universal tendency, therefore, is to assess others through the prism of one's own experience and to find other groups odd or deficient.

On occasion, some individuals may exhibit inverted ethnocentrism or reverse ethnocentrism. This is a preference for another group's lifestyle or values as compared to one's own. In such a case, individuals feel that another people's beliefs or customs are better than those of their own. For example, the members of some minority groups or ethnic groups may see the values of the dominant group in a society to be superior and preferable to that of their own parents. They may wish to rebel against customs and behavior that they consider to be embarrassing and old-fashioned.

Ethnocentrism is not necessarily bad, for it makes one aware of the strengths and the positive aspects of one's own way of life. It reinforces one's belief in the merits of one's own group and promotes social solidarity. On the other hand, even if one feels that one's lifestyle and ways are best, it is still desirable to practice cultural relativism. Cultural relativism recognizes the validity and dignity of diverse cultural traditions, even as one maintains a commitment to one's own. It accepts the idea of intercultural understanding and mutual respect. It avoids the fallacy of naive realism, the idea that people everywhere must interpret experience and behavior with the same cultural assumptions and premises.

Ethnocentrism carried to extremes can result in expressions of xenophobia, nativism, and racism. Xenophobia is a fear and strong dislike of strangers and foreigners. As an emotional and highly charged response, it can lead to hostile feelings and threatening actions against foreigners and immigrants. Nativism is closely related and is the desire to preserve a nostalgic past and an idealized society by restricting or excluding immigrants. Finally, racism is the belief that the race or physical characteristics of a group are responsible for its social inferiority or subordinate status.

Prejudice

As a negative attitude towards a category of people, prejudice is often communicated through mechanisms such as ethnic slurs, ethnic humor, popular culture, and the media. Ethnic slurs are derogatory terms used by the members of one racial or ethnic group to describe the members of another. Thus, the Irish may be disparagingly referred to as "a bunch of drunken Catholics" while Jews are labeled "bloodthirsty Shylocks out to get their pound of flesh." African Americans may be dismissed as "jungle bunnies" or "oversexed niggers" while Chinese are summarily tagged as "miserly Ching-Chong Chinamen."

Stereotypes are generalizations about a particular group. In stereotypical thinking, undesirable traits and attributes possessed by some individuals within a group are fallaciously assigned to all the members of that group. As a result, misleading or deceptive images of entire categories of people gain wide acceptance. People who accept stereotypes may believe that Poles are "big, stupid, and greasy" while Italians "smell of garlic breath and are tied to the Mafia." Japanese are "hardworking but sneaky" while Mexicans are "too busy having babies and living on welfare to work." Stereotypes fail to reckon with the reality that people are individuals. Few may stop to think that there are Jewish mothers who do not like chicken soup or that there are African Americans who do not enjoy dining on chitlins and okra.

Ethnic humor depicts the foibles of racial or ethnic groups by keying on stereotypes or cultural practices. Humor exists cross-

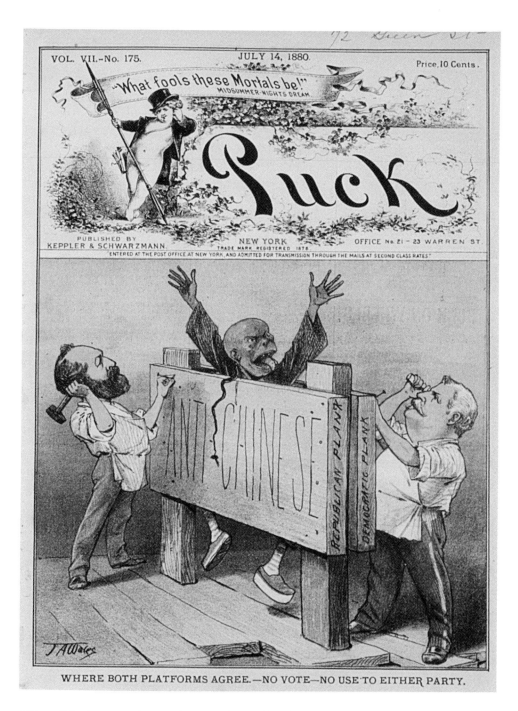

This political cartoon depicts the cynical attitude of both the Republican and the Democratic party during the period of the anti-Chinese movement. (Library of Congress)

culturally in all societies and functions as an art form and as a release for societal tensions. American society with its many immigrant and ethnic groups is particularly rich with ethnic humor. But jokes and caricatures about an ethnic group can lead to anger and bitterness if not delivered with sensitivity and in the proper context. Under the wrong circumstances, ethnic humor may serve to reinforce unfavorable stereotypes. Moreover, if subordinate groups are always the targets of ethnic humor while dominant groups are doing all the laughing, the result will be increased bitterness and misunderstanding.

Popular culture includes games, riddles, nursery rhymes, jump rope schemes, and songs. These forms of recreation and amusement have been dubbed the "secret world of children." In these vehicles for play, children often acquire important information that prepares them for the adult world. The values and beliefs expressed in their songs and games mirror those of the adult world. For example, in the streets of Hawaii there is a children's rhyme that goes: "One, two, three, bumblebees; who's the lady with the big chi-chi's?" "Chi-chi's" translates as breasts. It is doubtful if children at a youthful age are overly concerned with female breasts, but the adult preoccupation with this portion of female anatomy has somehow reflected itself in children's folklore. Other rhymes may embody prejudice. Thus, one popular jingle is recited:

> Eeny, meeny, miney, moe,
> Catch a nigger by the toe.
> If he hollers, let him go.
> My mother told me to choose this very one.
> O-u-t spells out goes he,
> Right in the middle of the deep, blue sea.

In the Civil Rights era, concerned parents sometimes told their children to delete the word "nigger" and to substitute "monkey" or "tiger" instead.

Lastly, the media in its many forms can disseminate stereotypes and reinforce prejudice. Comics, magazines, newspapers, tabloids, popular novels, advertisements, radio, television, and the movies constantly present new material to their audiences and publics. Many movies portray ethnic communities as characterized by urban violence. Ghetto life, gang warfare, family strife, and inner-city crime are common themes. Television programs about African Americans depict adult women as strong, independent, and the heads of families, while the men are weak, indecisive, and anxiety-ridden. Good role models for minorities are scarce because writers, producers, and the media provide few opportunities for minority actors in nonstereotypical scripts. The mass media often prefers to cater to a hypothetical majority and ignores or disregards minority viewers. To the extent that individuals in the audience may not be personally acquainted with minority persons, stereotypes presented in the media can reinforce existing prejudices or even contribute to new ones.

Discrimination

Discrimination can be contrasted with prejudice by defining it as action as opposed to attitude or belief. More precisely, it is action against a subordinate group that limits its rights and opportunities in the society. Discrimination makes distinctions against another group and denies it equal treatment and full enjoyment of its societal privileges.

Although many people assume that prejudice causes discrimination, that may not always be the case. Prejudice can occur without discrimination, while discrimination can take place for reasons other than prejudice. Thus, in the first case, people have a negative opinion of another group, but they do not follow through in their actions. In the second case, individuals may discriminate against a groupnot because of their own prejudices, but because of peer pressure and a desire to conform to escape attention. In fact, discriminatory actions can precede prejudice, as the latter later arises to rationalize or legitimize behavior already undertaken.

Just as prejudice has many guises, discrimination has many forms. At one level, verbal abuse, epithets, and other forms of expression may be directed at a target group. Insults, taunting, name-calling, and hostile graffiti writing can take place. Although everyone is familiar with the phrase "sticks and stones may break my bones but names will never hurt me," words can still inflict pain. At the second level, members of a dominant group may desire to avoid face-to-face interaction or other social contact with the members of a subordinate group. They may move to the suburbs, or they may seek to enroll their children in private schools.

The next level includes exclusion of a subordinate group from housing, employment, education, and social organizations. Segregation is practiced either formally or informally. The fourth level is physical abuse, with intimidation and organized violence being carried out. There may be beatings, attacks, mob actions, and other types of aggression. The fifth level is extermination, with genocide, massacres, or pogroms being conducted against a people. And yet, this list is hardly exhaustive. A subordinate group may not be allowed to testify in court, may not be permitted to vote, may be denied immigration rights, may be subjected to alien land laws, or may be discriminated against in anti-miscegenation laws, laws that forbid interracial marriage. For the Japanese in the United States, their experience included imprisonment in internment camps during World War II.

Exactly why prejudice and discrimination take place in various societies has been the topic of intensive examination. One theory suggests that it may be due to economic competition. A second theory attempts to account for it by focusing on the socialization in a society or how children learn. A third explanation states that it may be due to situational pressures or the responses triggered by specific settings. Still another view suggests that frustrated individuals seek to compensate for their own failure and powerlessness by belittling or attacking a targeted group. In short, the sources for prejudice and discrimination are many and complex.

Reducing Prejudice and Discrimination

Given that situation, one naturally wonders if there are ways to reduce prejudice and discrimination. One strategy is to emphasize education. People who are prejudiced and who practice discrimination often selectively learn information for their own purposes. They have an emotional screen that permits them to emphasize only that which they prefer to recall. In contrast, a program of multicultural education can help to foster intergroup understanding, instilling an awareness of the richness of diverse cultural traditions even as it underscores people's common humanity.

A second approach is to increase the opportunities for intergroup contact. Encouragement of face-to-face contact and interaction among people of different backgrounds can help to remove barriers to communication. It can help to foster empathy and an ability to see things from another person's viewpoint. Above all, people can learn to appreciate others as individuals with their distinctive personal qualities and merits instead of merely categorizing them into stereotyped groups.

Finally, a third method is to use the law and government to eliminate prejudice and discrimination. In the past, it was argued that laws and statutes could not erase folkways or popular mores. But governmental policy and laws can definitely eliminate certain practices or behaviors that are discriminatory to groups and individuals in American society. Moreover, once it is understood that certain actions will not be tolerated or acceptable, new norms and different attitudes become incorporated into everyday lives.

The reduction of prejudice and discrimination appears to be a daunting task. And yet, history has given cause for optimism. In the first two hundred years of the United States, there was a remarkable record of struggle for freedom, liberty, equality, and high ideals. Yet there has also been a dark side to American history, seen in the enslavement of Africans, the dispossession of Indians from their lands, and the persecution of religious dissenters. In the early part of this nation's past, nativist politicians and xenophobic agitators attacked Catholics, Jews, Asians, and immigrants from Eastern and Southern Europe. But slavery has been abolished, and segregation has been declared illegal. In recent decades, America has once again opened its doors to peoples and refugees from far flung corners of the globe. Education, increased intergroup contact, and a supportive legal environment have been largely responsible.

Still, the campaign against prejudice and discrimination has to be renewed for each generation. One need only look at the mixture of populations in the schools. Schools are a reflection of America in miniature; their students are a mirror of the diversity of the larger society. In the backgrounds and nationalities of the children, whether newcomers or residents, is the underlying reality that the United States is a cultural mosaic, a veritable "nation of nations." As children join together at play in the schoolgrounds, there may be harmony or there may be dissension. There may be prejudice and discrimination that reflect the stresses and strains of the larger society.

With each generation of youth, America reinvents itself. Today's young people are an America in process, a future waiting to be realized. They can embody the highest ideals, hopes, and aspirations of the American dream. Or they can repeat the dark side of American history. What will be the future?

2 The Chinese American Experience

"Yum sui si yuen . . . When drinking water, think of the source." So goes a popular Chinese saying. In recent years as the Chinese population in America has grown dramatically, greater interest has surfaced in learning about the roots of its early communities in this country. New Chinese historical societies have been established, and new publications treat different aspects of the rich Chinese American past.

Early Period

The Chinese who arrived in America in the mid-nineteenth century came because of a combination of push and pull factors. The push factors were considerations that made it advantageous to leave the homeland. Such factors included population pressure, interethnic conflict, foreign wars, and political unrest. The pull factors were attractions that drew them to this country. The wide, unsettled West with its vast need for human labor was one consideration. The other enticement was the discovery of gold at John Sutter's mill in California in 1848. To this day, the Chinese continue to refer to California as "Gum Shan" or the "Gold Mountain."

In departing from their homeland, those who went to the United States were part of a large overseas diaspora, or dispersal, of Chinese. Seeking ways to improve their livelihood, many had emigrated to Hawaii, Southeast Asia, and the Americas. Most of those who came to Hawaii and the West Coast left from Kwangtung province, a region with centuries of experience in shipping and foreign trade. More informed than most Chinese about countries outside China, the Cantonese were naturally more receptive to the idea of emigration.

California and the West Coast of the United States proved to be an attractive destination. Wonderful opportunities seemed to be in store for those who dared to cross the blue waters of the Pacific Ocean. In this respect, the Chinese were no different from many other Argonauts who traveled in search of gold to California in 1849. Hawaiians, Latin Americans, Europeans, and Chinese belonged to a common fraternity as soldiers of fortune. The idea that everyone would soon become wealthy was captured in the phrase "Gum Shan Hak Mou Yut Chin You Bat Bak." Translated, the saying suggested that "A guest of Gold Mountain who did not return with one thousand dollars, was bound to return with eight hundred."

In America, the Chinese found the chances for employment to be abundant. Mining was one of the most popular occupations, and Chinese prospectors fanned out throughout the American West in quest of the precious metals. Their presence in many Western locales was acknowledged with place names such as "Chinese Camp" and "China Slide." The construction of the transcontinental railroad in the 1860's and other railways of the late nineteenth century also provided the Chinese with steady employment. Still others worked in agriculture, helping to clear the land, building irrigation canals, and draining wet swamplands. Aware of the crops that could be planted in the new setting, the Chinese introduced vegetables and fruits that can now be found in supermarkets.

Fishing was a common livelihood in South China, and the Chinese understood that there was a rich bounty that could be

Traditional values and attitudes remain influential among Chinese Americans today. (Richard Hutchings/InfoEdit)

harvested from the sea. They pioneered in the development of the great West Coast fishing industry along with the later Japanese, Portuguese, and Italians, who also labored in that line of work. They dried, preserved, and pickled fish, shellfish, seaweed, and other foods from the ocean for export back to Asia.

The Chinese also opened factories and industries. In San Francisco, they assembled cigars and manufactured woolen garments, shoes, candles, jute bags, and other articles. In addition, some Chinese opened restaurants, served as gardeners, and worked as domestic servants. In short, the Chinese discovered a labor shortage and were able to specialize in many forms of employment.

Anti-Chinese Sentiment

Immigrants have frequently been the targets of attacks by members of the host society. The Chinese were no different. As immigrants from Asia, they were singled out by nativists for being physically different and for practicing different customs. Labor leaders saw them as a source of competition and urged workers to join together to protect their interests. Difficult economic times only exacerbated the situation and increased the potential for violence and prejudicial acts.

In the nineteenth century, the Chinese were the focus of many discriminatory laws and measures at the state and local level. Attempts were made to deny them residence, economic livelihood, and legal protection in the courts. Because China was a weak nation and had been defeated by European nations in war, Chinese officials were not able to protect their subjects in the United States. Washington could easily disregard the pleas and protests of an ineffectual government. "Not a Chinaman's chance" was an apt description of the fact that it was open season upon Chinese, who were fair game for violence and hostility. Beatings, killings, massacres, lynchings, and expulsions were common occurrences in the nineteenth century.

In 1882, Congress passed the Chinese Exclusion Act and prohibited the entry of Chinese male laborers for ten years. The act was a humiliating measure, for it marked China as being the first nation to ever be denied immigration to the United States. In 1892 and 1902, the law was renewed, and in 1904, the exclusion was made permanent. First-generation Chinese were also denied naturalization and could not become American citizens, regardless of their length of residence in the United States. Thus, they could not vote.

Barred from full participation in American society, members of the Chinese community reacted in various ways. Some returned to China, feeling that the United States would never extend them hospitality and full acceptance. Others moved to the Eastern part of the United States and to Hawaii, where it was hoped anti-Chinese sentiment would be less visible. Large numbers, however, chose to remain on the West Coast and withdrew into Chinatowns, in which they might be able to avoid scrutiny and hostility.

Community Organization

Within their own communities, the Chinese organized associations and societies. These groups offered membership based on family affiliation, geographical region, occupation, and other shared interests. The Sam Yup Association, for example, was a society based upon geography. The term "Sam Yup" means "Three Districts." This organization included Cantonese who were from the Namhoi, Punyu, and Shuntak sections of the Pearl River delta in Kwangtung province. Similar to most immigrant societies, it provided friendship, assistance, financial support, translation, and other essential services that helped in the adaptation to an alien land.

To foster cooperation among the many regional groups, Chinatowns also featured a "Chung Wah Wui Goon" or Chinese Consolidated Benevolent Association . Whereas the other

From the time of the first immigrants to the present, Chinese Americans have shown a strong sense of community. (Robert Brenner/PhotoEdit)

organizations divided people according to dialect, surname, region, or occupation, the Chinese Consolidated Benevolent Association sought to promote unity and cooperation. An omnibus organization that claimed to represent all the people of the Chinese community, it mediated disputes, coordinated policy, and resolved problems that affected the welfare of all. Outsiders often did not understand the function of this society, and they simply referred to it as the "Six Companies." The head of the Six Companies was frequently assumed to be the "Mayor of Chinatown."

Temples, altars, and churches also were to be found in Chinatowns. Like other immigrant groups, the Chinese held dear the philosophies and religions of their ancestral homeland. Many practiced an eclectic mix of Buddhism and Taoism, still popular among Chinese believers today. Others had already been Christians in China or had converted to Christianity in the United States. These individuals attended mission churches established to minister to their needs, or they later went to immigrant or ethnic Chinese Christian churches.

In the period before World War II, Chinese communities were primarily bachelor societies. As sojourners who planned to return to China to live, many Chinese did not bring their wives with them to the United States. Moreover, the exclusionary immigration laws prevented women from joining potential husbands. As a result, those families that were fortunate to be in America and that had children were the envy of the community. Their children were surrounded by loving "uncles" who showered them with sweets, candies,and presents.

These children became the foundation of the second generation. Unlike the first generation, those who were born on American soil could claim U.S. citizenship under the Constitution. Able to vote and fully conscious of their status as American citizens, they could participate more completely in the larger society. They were also the window to change. By attending public schools, eating American food, reading newspapers, and viewing movies, they could interpret the larger society for their parents.

During World War II, China became a wartime ally of the United States in the conflict against Japan. Many Chinese in this country volunteered to fight in the American war effort. Because of friendly feelings for a comrade-in-arms, Congress effected changes in immigration policy for China. In 1943, China was given a quota of 105 persons per year. Moreover, Chinese of the first generation were finally permitted to receive citizenship through naturalization. Now the parents could join their children in reaping the full benefits of American citizenship.

The postwar years brought further changes for Chinese Americans. The economic growth and affluence of postwar America allowed many Chinese to attain middle-class status. Liberalized immigration laws, particularly in 1965, redressed past inequities and permitted larger quotas for Chinese to enter the United States. Family unification became possible, and the Chinese community became a family society instead of a bachelor society.

In addition, new life was brought to Chinese communities in Chinatowns and the suburbs. The demography of the new immigration has meant less concentration of population in the inner cities and the West Coast states. Today, rapidly growing Chinese communities may be found in the Midwest, the South, and the East Coast. At the same time, the old residential areas have benefited from the vitality and dynamism of the new immigrant populations.

In many respects, the Chinese American population is no longer as homogeneous as in the past. New immigrants, who constitute the majority of the Chinese American population, now come from Hong Kong, Taiwan, mainland China, Singapore, and Southeast Asia. Many speak Mandarin and other dialects different from the Cantonese spoken by the nineteenth century immigrants. For this reason, older immigrant and ethnic community organizations may have difficulty in accommodating the new populations. Intraethnic conflicts and tensions may arise.

Recent Period

Many Chinese find it troubling that they are now described as a "Model Minority." The term itself hides the prejudice and the discrimination that they encountered in the past. Furthermore, the phrase disguises the social problems and the growing pains that the Chinese American community must confront. Growing numbers of elderly, juvenile delinquency and gang activity, limited English proficiency, housing, employment, and a resurgence in anti-Asian violence are some of the issues that need to be addressed.

On balance, however, Chinese Americans take pride in the achievements and successes registered by their community. The academic excellence of Chinese American students in schools and universities has received national attention in recent years. Scientists and educators have won acclaim for their important discoveries and contributions. Professionals and entrepreneurs have won kudos for their impressive records. Finally, Chinese American writers and artists have expanded awareness on the part of the larger society regarding the diversity and creativity of the Chinese American community. Their efforts have helped to destroy existing stereotypes about Chinese Americans as a monolithic and homogeneous group, even as they provide audiences with exciting and novel forms of literary and cultural expression.

Chinese Americans are strongly committed to education. (Mary Kate Denny/ PhotoEdit)

Along with the many social and demographic changes in the Chinese American population, the question of Chinese American identity is also undergoing change. Before World War II, many Chinese in the United States referred to themselves as "Chinese" or "Orientals." Many saw themselves as sojourners, destined to return to China. For the moment, they were overseas Chinese in America.

World War II and the Civil Rights era brought about key changes. The new changes in immigration policy and laws introduced a new consciousness. Many now no longer saw themselves as overseas Chinese or sojourners. They could now be American citizens. In the 1960's, Chinese Americans also adopted new labels for themselves. They now choose to be called "Chinese Americans" rather than "Chinese." Moreover, instead of using the word "Oriental," they promote the use of the term "Asian American."

The coining and currency of these new terms is more than a fad. The words indicate a new confidence, a new assertiveness, and a new identity. Many Chinese Americans have discovered an exhilaration and a sense of exuberance in assuming a pan-Asian American identity. They enjoy the stimulation and feeling of solidarity in joining with the causes of other Asian Americans in the United States.

But can a Chinese American identity and a pan-Asian American identity coexist? Is it possible for Chinese Americans to assume both identities? The current pattern suggests change and fluidity, and the contemporary situation poses challenges as well as novel opportunities. Asian Americans in the United States may be undergoing a process of redefining themselves and building new group identities. The future is far from clear, but the possibilities are exciting.

3 Immigration and Reception

Migration, or the movement of peoples, is one of the important themes in world history, but it is often neglected because of a tendency to focus on political units such as nations and states. Migration is due to a combination of push and pull factors. Push factors are those domestic reasons that encourage people to leave their homeland. Pull factors are external reasons that attract people to another destination or host country.

Factors in Immigration

For the Chinese in the mid-nineteenth century, there were four push factors. One was population increase. In 1600 the population of China was 130 million; by 1850 it had risen to 430 million. The growth was fostered by the introduction of new plants and foods from the Americas. Maize or corn, the white and sweet potato, peanuts, and tobacco, were among the crops that increased the food supply for China. But by the nineteenth century, the dramatic growth in population had outstripped the gains in agriculture. Drought, flooding, rebellions, and wars could only worsen the situation by disrupting food production.

A second factor was interethnic conflict. The Hakka or "guest people" were Chinese from the north who had migrated to Kwangtung province along the southeastern coast of China. Their movement placed them in conflict with the people who had long been established in that region, the Punti, or "local people." The groups competed for land, water, and other resources, and war actually occurred between the Hakka and the Punti. Moreover, differences in dialect and customs intensified the gulf between the two groups. For the most part, the Punti prevailed in the rivalry and the Hakka found themselves forced into the mountainous and less fertile areas where it was harder to make a living.

A third reason was conflict between China and the West. In the latter part of the nineteenth century, a series of wars were fought between China and the West. Europe had long valued products from China such as tea, porcelain, silk, cotton textiles,

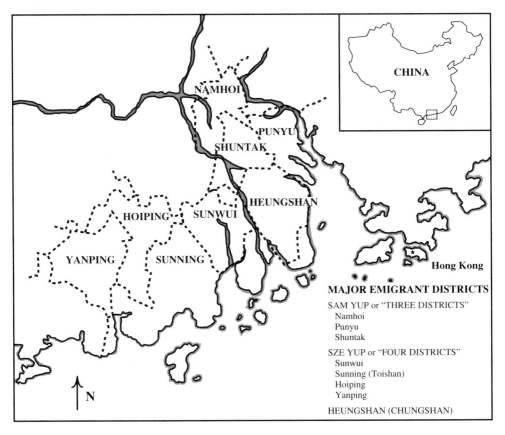

and furniture. The Chinese permitted trading at the port of
Canton in Kwangtung province, but they desired nothing from
the West. The result was a negative balance of trade for the
European countries and the United States as specie, that is,
money in coin, and silver was paid to China.

To stem the drain of precious metals, the countries trading
with China experimented with a variety of products. For
example, furs from the Pacific Northwest of North America were
sold to the Chinese, but the hunting rapidly depleted the animal
population. Sandalwood in the Hawaiian Islands was known to be
prized by the Chinese for its special fragrance, and it was used in
the manufacture of fans, furniture, and other items. But
continued shipment of the wood to China resulted in
deforestation. Today the Chinese still refer to Hawaii as "Tan
Heung Shan," which means the "Sandalwood mountains," but
the few sandalwood extant there are only to be found in a
botanical garden. Bêche-de-mer or sea cucumber harvested from
the sea was considered a culinary delicacy in China, but it could
not be extracted in large enough quantities to pay for the
commodities desired by the West.

Not until opium was sold to China was there a reversal in the
terms of trade. The British East India Company had discovered
that opium processed from poppies in India could be marketed in
Canton. The Chinese had traditionally used opium as a medicine,
and some smoked it as a pastime. But opium was also a narcotic,
and as growing numbers of Chinese indulged in the habit, the
Emperor Yung-cheng banned the sale and smoking of opium in
1729. In 1796 the Emperor Chia-ch'ing prohibited the cultivation
of opium and its importation from other lands.

Nevertheless, the traffic in opium was too profitable to be
ignored. Local officials, Chinese merchants, and foreign
businessmen disregarded the laws and continued to trade in
opium. The growing opium traffic eventually led to trade deficits
and an outflow of Chinese silver. When the Chinese government
initiated a policy of strict prohibition and seized British opium,
the action precipitated a war. Great Britain had found Chinese

trade restrictions unacceptable, and it welcomed the opportunity to redress the situation. In the Opium War that followed from 1839 to 1842, China was defeated, and it had to agree to the provisions specified in the Treaty of Nanking. Hong Kong Island was ceded to the British, and an indemnity had to be paid. Moreover, five ports had to be opened for trade; they were Canton, Shanghai, Amoy, Ningpo, and Foochow. Canton's trade monopoly with the West was ended, and Kwangtung experienced competition from the other ports and the loss of jobs. China reluctantly accepted these terms and tried to resist additional changes in its foreign relations with the West. The consequences were predictable; there were further conflicts and other wars were fought.

A fourth cause of Chinese migration was political disorder. The Ch'ing dynasty was in the throes of dynastic decline, and the empire ruled by the Manchus was characterized by corruption, governmental ineffectiveness, and peasant unrest. The demographic pressures and foreign wars merely aggravated the situation. The Taiping Rebellion, led by a Hakka leader named Hung Hsiu-ch'uan, broke out between 1850 and 1864. The rebels struggling against the government ravaged the countryside, and an estimated ten to twenty million people died in the upheaval. At the same time, other revolts such as the Nien and Moslem Rebellions also flared up. In Kwangtung province, an insurrection mounted by rebels named the Red Turbans also erupted in 1854 and 1855.

Faced with these domestic crises, the Chinese were attracted to the United States by two pull factors. One was the discovery of gold in California on land owned by John Augustus Sutter in 1848. As news of the discovery spread, people from all over the world came to prospect for gold. The Chinese were similar in this respect; they shared in the optimism of the Argonauts that quick wealth could be found in California.

A second pull factor was the opportunity for employment in the United States. The West Coast was still thinly settled, and laborers were needed in many occupations. Life in a strange land

A Chinese New Year parade; this holiday, which falls later than January 1, is celebrated by people of Chinese descent throughout the world. (Susan Hormuth)

might be difficult, but the chances for making a living seemed comparatively better than that available in a China beset by internal turmoil and foreign conflict. They could save their earnings and send remittances home to their relatives. Should luck favor them, they could return home after several years and purchase land or start a business. Surrounded by family and friends, they could then lead a comfortable life as a reward for their hard work abroad.

Sources of Immigration

In less troubled times, Kwangtung province was considered a rich food-producing region. Its warm, subtropical climate blessed with abundant rainfall meant that there was a yearlong growing season, permitting double cropping or even triple cropping. Mulberry trees, rice, tea, sugar cane, and vegetables flourished in the setting. Lichee, pomelos, mangoes, plums, peaches, guavas, persimmons, and pineapples were among the fruits that were harvested. Livestock such as pigs, chickens, ducks, and fish were also raised for food. Because of the diversity of foods enjoyed in

Kwangtung, Cantonese food was deemed to be the premier regional cuisine in China. As a well-known Chinese proverb proclaimed, "One should be born in Soochow, eat in Kwangchow (Canton), live in Hangchow, and die in Liuchow."

The confluence of factors that caused instability, internal rebellion, and foreign conflict also affected Kwangtung province. The Cantonese had a history of overseas settlement and commerce with Southeast Asia, and their merchants had engaged in trade with the West. More familiar with the outside world, the Cantonese were readier to emigrate during hard times than were most of their countrymen. The major source of Chinese immigrants to America was a small region made up of eight districts of the Pearl River delta in Kwangtung province. The Chinese themselves refer to these eight districts as the Sam Yup, Chungshan, and Sze Yup areas.

The Sam Yup or "Three Districts" area is made up of three districts located to the west of Canton, the capital of Kwangtung. Punyu, Namhoi, and Shuntak were collectively an economic region that specialized in agriculture, commerce, and the production of silk and pottery. 17 percent of the Chinese who emigrated to the United States in the 1850's came from Sam Yup. Immigrants from these three districts became some of the important merchants, tailors, butchers, and factory owners in San Francisco.

The Chungshan district, formerly known as Heungshan, is situated to the southwest of Canton and is close to the Portuguese colony of Macao. Its economy consisted of agriculture, fishing, handicrafts, and commerce. In the 1850's, people from this district accounted for one-third of the Chinese population in the United States. In Hawaii, they comprised about 75 to 80 percent of the Chinese population. In California, immigrants from Chungshan were well represented in farming, truck gardening, plant nurseries, and retail businesses.

The Sze Yup or "Four Districts" area includes Sunwui, Hoiping, Yanping, and Toishan, formerly known as Sunning. Situated to the west of Chungshan, the Sze Yup area has more hilly terrain and less arable land, so its people are less well off than those from the other four districts. Agriculture and fishing formed the dominant means of livelihood for this region. Migrants from Sze Yup were the largest group among the Chinese in the United States in the 1850's. Prior to the new wave of immigration that began in the mid-1960's, people who traced their descent to the Sze Yup area made up 70 percent of the Chinese population in the United States. In California, many of the immigrants from Sze Yup worked as laborers, domestic servants, and laundrymen.

Journeying Across the Pacific

When the Manchus conquered China in 1644, they enacted policies to discourage emigration overseas. Chinese supporters of the previous Ming dynasty had fled to Southeast Asia and Taiwan, hoping to maintain resistance against the alien Ch'ing dynasty. Fearing these Ming loyalists, the Manchu government saw overseas Chinese as potential enemies and traitors opposed to its rule. As a result, it imposed a harsh penalty of death upon those who traveled abroad. But the difficulty of consolidating control over a large empire meant that its enforcement was less than successful, especially in southeastern China, where people continued to seek jobs and to trade in neighboring countries as in centuries past. In the nineteenth century, the internal problems and external challenges further eroded imperial control against Chinese emigration.

The Chinese immigrants who journeyed to the United States financed their passage across the Pacific by various means. Some immigrants could afford to pay the fare themselves. Another alternative was to utilize the credit-ticket system. Money was borrowed for the fare from a broker, merchant, or employer. After arriving in America, the person would gradually repay the debt while working. A third was the contract labor system. Under this means, a person worked for a period to repay the debt to the employer who had provided his fare. The method was similar to the indentured servant status that early colonists had used to secure passage to America. A last way was to mortgage one's land or property or to get a loan for the ship's fare. Of the four

San Francisco's Chinatown, the first center of Chinese immigration and still a major cultural center for Chinese Americans. (Deborah Davis/PhotoEdit)

methods employed, the one most commonly used appears to have been the credit-ticket system.

Negative Perceptions of China and the Chinese

Two developments that coincided with the arrival of Chinese immigrants in the United States, however, cast shadows over their acceptance. One was China's military weakness, and the second was the coolie trade. Before its defeat in the Opium War, China had commanded respect in the West as a rich and powerful civilization. But the victory by Great Britain shattered that image. Subsequent defeats in the Second Opium War and the Sino-French War reinforced the perception that China was a weak nation.

The privileges that the unequal treaties conferred upon the West contributed to the impression that China was inferior. China had to make concessions infringing upon its sovereignty that were not reciprocated by the West. For example, extraterritoriality and international settlement areas in China gave foreigners immunity from Chinese law. Diplomats who had chafed at the ethnocentrism of Chinese diplomatic etiquette now spoke of a haughty empire brought to its knees. Traders who formerly had acquiesced to Chinese trade restrictions now complained about the corruption in Chinese business practices. Soldiers criticized the inadequacy of Chinese military preparations and tactics, while missionaries talked about the superstitions and pagan beliefs of the Chinese people. Travelers who toured the Chinese countryside wrote back home about the polygamy, poverty, and filth in China.

The defeat of China by Japan in the Sino-Japanese War of 1894 to 1895 surprised the West even more. A smaller nation had been able to humiliate an empire many times its size. Japan had shown that it had been an apt pupil of the West; it had been a progressive nation capable of modernizing and industrializing. But China seemed to be hopeless. It was the "sick man of Asia," and Western nations embarked upon a drive to gain spheres of influence in China. Political pundits described this process as "the carving of the Chinese melon." Military weakness was increasingly equated with backwardness and cultural inferiority.

The second ominous development was the coolie trade. Great Britain and other European nations had ended their participation in slavery and the slave trade in the early part of the nineteenth century. But the result was a shortage of labor in Latin America, the Malay Archipelago, and the West Indies. Asian Indians and Chinese appeared to be suitable substitutes. Whether by deception or by force, thousands of Chinese were confined in holding areas called barracoons. Labor recruiters and ship captains then transported them to places where their labor was needed. A highly profitable trade in involuntary labor, the coolie traffic was rife with abuses. Mistreatment was common, conditions on the ships were appalling, and many of the coolies sent to work in Cuba and Peru perished.

In contrast, the Chinese who went to Australia, Canada, and the United States were not part of the coolie trade; they had voluntarily emigrated. Nevertheless, popular knowledge about the coolie traffic elsewhere placed a stigma upon Chinese laborers in the United States. Chinese laborers were presumed to be coolies, and the credit-ticket and contract labor systems of passage were often assumed to be identical with the coolie trade. Placed against a backdrop of an American Civil War recently fought over the question of slavery, the topic of coolies could provoke fiery debate. For some, it was all too easy to see the Chinese as docile slaves competing against free white labor. Coupled with a perception that China was backward and culturally inferior, it was not too difficult for others to see Chinese immigrants as benighted, servile labor.

Like other immigrants, the Chinese came to America with high hopes. If conditions were right, they could eke out a living, send money to relatives, and possibly even return home. But an unfavorable image of China and coolies would negatively affect their acceptance in the United States.

4 Employment and Competition

Mining

Many forms of employment were available to the Chinese immigrants soon after their arrival in California. One obvious choice was mining for gold, an enterprise that offered the hope of sudden wealth. After getting the necessary supplies from San Francisco, the Chinese moved into the interior. The popularity of a place with the Chinese was indicated by the name that they assigned it. Thus, San Francisco was called "Dai Fow" or the "Big City." Sacramento was "Yih Fow" or the "Second City," and Marysville was "Sam Fow" or the "Third City." Along with the other miners who had descended upon California, they wandered from site to site prospecting for gold. Pristine sites were not the only desirable locations; oftentimes abandoned claims were also considered suitable. While other miners hurried to places where new strikes had been discovered, the Chinese found that patience and hard work could extricate enough gold dust and nuggets to make old sites worthwhile.

Chinese encounters with other miners were sometimes unpleasant. The law was practically nonexistent on the mining frontier; people frequently made their own law. Claim jumping was seen as an abominable and unforgivable offense. Prospectors were so intent on getting rich that greed, ambition, and jealousy fostered bitter disputes. Believing that the Chinese did not deserve to share in California's wealth, other miners sometimes drove them away from gold sites. One illustration might suffice. A group of miners came upon a party of Chinese panning for gold and evicted them. The Chinese exclaimed, "I go," hoping to avoid a violent confrontation. When they moved to another site, another group likewise forced them out. Unhappy at this repetition of their previous encounter, the dejected Chinese cried out, "Oh, no!" If we can believe the gazetteers that list California place-names and their origins, that is how the mining towns of Igo and Ono got their name.

By the 1860's, the surface veins of gold were exhausted. Mining was entering a new phase, a corporate phase. The exploitation of deeper veins or deposits required expensive equipment and skilled labor. Miners who relied upon panning or rocker cradling were slowly being replaced by larger corporate concerns that could marshal huge amounts of capital, hire mining experts, and purchase costly equipment. At this juncture, many Chinese were able to turn to the railroads for employment.

Railroads

In 1862, the Congress and President Abraham Lincoln had authorized construction of a transcontinental railroad that could link the East and the West. Besides curbing sectionalism, it could improve communication, transportation, and commerce among different regions of the country. Moreover, some industrialists hoped that the line could promote the shipment of Eastern manufactures and goods to the markets of Asia. Two railroad companies were to cooperate in the project. From the West, the Central Pacific Railroad would build eastward from Sacramento, California. In the East, the Union Pacific Railroad would build westward from Omaha, Nebraska.

The Civil War hampered the undertaking. Large numbers of men had joined to fight in the Union or Confederate armies in the East. Others saw railroading as backbreaking work that was too difficult. On January 8, 1863, Governor Leland Stanford of

California had broken ground for the Central Pacific Railroad at K Street in Sacramento. Two years later, in 1865, a scant 31 miles of track had been laid. The major problem was a labor shortage. In the East, the Union Pacific Railroad faced a similar dilemma.

Charles Crocker, a superintendent for the Central Pacific Railroad, suggested the use of Chinese laborers for construction work. At first the idea was ridiculed, but eventually the experiment was reluctantly acceded to. The trial proved to be successful; the fifty Chinese who had been hired showed themselves to be reliable and hardworking. As a result, more Chinese were recruited. At one point, as many as 10,000 to 12,000 Chinese were employed by the Central Pacific. For its part, the Union Pacific also relied on immigrants, such as the Irish and other Europeans.

Because Charles Crocker had hired the Chinese, they were sometimes called "Crocker's Pets." Observers generally agreed that the Chinese, who were organized into gangs of twelve to twenty members, were conscientious and good workers. But the Chinese were far from docile. On occasion, insensitivity and harsh working conditions led the Chinese to ask for better treatment. In the winter of 1866, for example, the Chinese were ordered to persevere and to accelerate their efforts despite the bitter cold and heavy snowdrifts. This assault on the high Sierra Nevadas during one of the coldest winters on record resulted in many lives being lost. In the following year, the Chinese struck and demanded a raise in wages and an eight-hour day. But Charles Crocker cut off their food supply, other workers did not provide support, and so the strike collapsed.

When the transcontinental railroad was completed in 1869, some Chinese worked on other trunk and branch lines. They helped to build the Southern Pacific Railroad, which linked Los Angeles to New Orleans. They also worked on the Northern Pacific Railroad, which connected Portland, Oregon, to Lake Superior. A few rugged and daring Chinese even moved to Canada and Mexico, helping to lay track and to build railways there. Still others left railroading after the transcontinental railroad was finished and worked as migrant laborers, tenant farmers, or gardeners.

Agriculture

In the vast, largely unsettled West, labor was a scarce commodity. People were able to find less arduous work that paid higher wages than farming. But with the completion of the transcontinental railroad, many Chinese were available for employment in agriculture. Farmers hired them to plant and to harvest crops and vegetables. Thus, the Chinese helped with crops such as wheat, cotton, sugar beets, hops, and strawberries. Agoston Haraszthy, the father of California viticulture, brought the Chinese to northern California vineyards in the 1860's, employing a hundred of them at the rate of one dollar a day. Other vineyards followed suit and hired Chinese workers; before long, the Chinese could be found in the Napa, Sonoma, and even Central California vineyards. In the fruit orchards, the Chinese helped to harvest apples, peaches, cherries, pears, and olives. They also dried raisins, figs, and fruits. Still others joined in land reclamation to drain swampland, while some helped to build irrigation canals and levees.

In addition, having come from the rich agricultural area of the Pearl River delta in Kwangtung, the Chinese saw opportunities to introduce Chinese vegetables, fruits, and herbs, that later found their way to supermarkets and dining room tables. Chinese tenant farmers and land owners favored truck gardening, a practice that weaned California away from its prior emphasis on the planting of wheat. The numerous contributions of the Chinese to agriculture can be validated through many examples. For instance, the Bing cherry was named after a Chinese foreman who planted cherries in Milwaukie, Oregon. To cite another example, the American Pomological Society awarded its Wilder Medal to Lue Gim Gong in 1911. He had developed a variety of hardy orange that could withstand frosts and enable Florida to compete against the California citrus industry.

A merchant in San Francisco's Chinatown; wherever Chinese immigrants settled, Chinese businesses sprang up to serve them. (Vicki Silbert/PhotoEdit)

Inevitably there were Chinese Horatio Algers who prospered and became successful among their fellow immigrants. In the San Joaquin Valley, one individual, Chin Lung, became known as the "Chinese Potato King." Originally from Heungshan district in Kwangtung, he leased thousands of acres of land in the Sacramento-San Joaquin delta of California. Planting potatoes, onions, asparagus, beans, hay, and grain, he employed more than 500 Chinese employees. He also owned two barges to supply his workers with provisions and to ship his produce to San Francisco. When he finally retired and returned to China, he had invested his money in an import-export firm, a manufacturing company, and the Wing On Department Store in Shanghai.

Fishing

Kwangtung province is situated on the southeastern coast of China. Not surprisingly, Cantonese immigrants were aware of the wealth that could be harvested from the sea. Fish, shellfish, seaweed, and other edible items could be caught. If dried, salted, or preserved, they could be exported for sale to the markets of Asia. Consequently, in the nineteenth century, Chinese junks and other vessels sailed out to extract this rich bounty from the waters off the Pacific coast. In California, Chinese fishing camps were set up in places like San Francisco, Monterey, and San Diego. At San Rafael, California, several hundred residents lived and fished together at this site, which has now been designated a California state park.

Manufacturing

For the Chinese in San Francisco, manufacturing was also an important occupation. They are usually not associated with this form of employment, but in the nineteenth century, the Chinese were prominently represented in that line of work. San Francisco was the center of the cigar industry on the West Coast, and in 1866, the Chinese operated half of the cigar factories in that city. In 1870, they also owned eleven out of twelve factories that produced slippers, shoes, and boots. Aside from ownership, the Chinese worked in factories that produced woolen textiles, clothing, brooms, candles, jute bags, soap, matches, bottles, and pottery.

Other Employment

Wherever there were large numbers of Chinese, merchants and peddlers appeared to provide goods and services. For example, when Chinese miners went into the foothills to prospect for gold, enterprising entrepreneurs followed them. They established Chinese restaurants and groceries that catered to Chinese and non-Chinese alike. Although not a major occupation among the Chinese in Kwangtung, Chinese laundries sprang up in America to serve what was initially a male clientele. Still other Chinese immigrants worked as servants, houseboys, and cooks, providing domestic labor for those who were wealthy. In larger Chinese communities, businessmen started import-export stores, herbal shops, clothing stores, barber shops, groceries, bakeries, restaurants, produce stalls, and fish and livestock markets to serve the population.

Hawaii

Although the largest number of Chinese lived on the West Coast, they also resided in Hawaii and other parts of the country. In Hawaii, the Chinese had set foot in the Polynesian kingdom as early as 1789. After 1852, many found employment as contract laborers on the rice and sugar plantations of Hawaii. Finding conditions difficult with limited opportunities for upward mobility, they failed to renew their contracts and started their own farms or businesses. Others moved away from the rural areas to the larger towns and cities where they could be closer to other Chinese and the attractions of an urban life. Plantation owners increasingly considered the Chinese an unsatisfactory labor force, and they systematically recruited the Japanese as a replacement in the period after 1885.

The South

In the South, the emancipation of slaves after the Civil War resulted in a need for workers in the cotton fields. Southern plantation owners brought in Chinese laborers as a substitute in states such as Louisiana, Arkansas, and Mississippi. The experiment proved to be a failure, however, for the Chinese regarded the work as too tedious and demanding. Some relocated to the North or to the West, while a few remained and opened grocery stores. In the Pacific Northwest, the Midwest, and on the East Coast, the Chinese had advanced along with the various economic frontiers. Mining, railroading, and agriculture led to the dispersal of the Chinese as they fanned outward from San Francisco. But in general, most of the Chinese communities outside the West Coast were smaller and less populous.

Ominous Signs

Even before their arrival in the United States, the Chinese had been preceded by unfavorable images and negative stereotypes. China's humiliating defeat by Great Britain in the Opium War and the abuses of the coolie traffic tainted the Chinese with adverse publicity. While some individuals such as Governor John McDougal of California welcomed the Chinese for their labor and industry, others did not share that vision. As substantial numbers of Chinese immigrants appeared in California and the West Coast, expressions of ethnocentrism, nativism, and racism began to surface. For example, Governor John Bigler, McDougal's successor, warned in 1852 about the menacing tide of Chinese immigration to California. Hostile critics hurled epithets at the Chinese immigrants, describing them as a stagnant people and an inferior breed made up of "heathens," "debased coolies," and "addicted opium smokers."

As the Chinese entered into the different forms of employment, the opportunities for conflict increased. Miners, for instance, resented the presence of the Chinese in the gold country and viewed them with contempt. They banned the Chinese from some mining camps and forcefully expelled them from their claims. Thus, about three hundred Chinese miners were driven away from North Fork on the American River and others were evicted from sites in Shasta County in the 1850's. A report of a committee to the California state legislature in 1862 noted that many Chinese had been harassed, robbed, and murdered in the mining regions.

In other sectors of the economy, labor leaders, workers, and their supporters feared that the Chinese might drive down wages or might be used as strikebreakers. Terence Powderly of the Knights of Labor, Samuel Gompers of the American Federation of Labor, Eugene V. Debs, and Henry George were all spokesmen for labor and severe critics of the Chinese as unwelcome immigrants. In San Francisco, anti-coolie clubs were organized as early as 1862 to alert people about the threat of cheap Chinese labor. Similar clubs were later formed in other cities and states as workers became alarmed about the possibility of competition from Chinese labor. In San Francisco itself, labor leaders and union members tried to expel Chinese immigrants from the cigar factories, the shoe and boot trades, and other industries. Furthermore, whenever recessions or depressions occurred from the 1870's to the 1890's, the Chinese became convenient scapegoats for the loss of jobs and the drop in wages. Life and labor for the Chinese immigrants in "Gold Mountain" was clearly not going to be easy and uneventful.

5 The Anti-Chinese Movement

Causes

Although Chinese immigrants had contributed significantly to the development of the American West, a virulent anti-Chinese movement soon began to take shape. Several reasons may be cited as being responsible for this situation. First, the West as a frontier region was a relatively unsettled area. Lacking legal and educational institutions and marked by a relative scarcity of women, the West was easily prone to violence. Vigilante justice and intolerant demands for group conformity were common. In such a raw, untamed environment, prejudice and racism fused easily with nativism and xenophobia. Physically distinct and characterized by different cultural practices, the Chinese were readily noticed and targeted. The "Chinese problem" on the West Coast became the equivalent of the "colored problem" focused on blacks in the South.

A second factor was the perception that the Chinese were competing for the jobs of white workers. The labor leader Samuel Gompers authored a pamphlet entitled *Some Reasons for Chinese Exclusion: Meat vs. Rice, American Manhood against Coolieism—Which Shall Survive?* (1908). As the title graphically indicates, many Americans saw Chinese immigrants as threatening rivals. As president of the American Federation of Labor, Gompers actively argued for the exclusion of the Chinese from the United States and refused to permit them to join any chapter of his union. Other labor leaders and workers shared similar concerns. In many cases, these fears combined with blatant prejudice and unbridled xenophobia. This formed a volatile mix, and West Coast leaders seized upon the anti-Chinese theme as a catalyst to help them build a strong union movement.

A third cause was the economic changes that had been taking place. The West was undergoing a dramatic transformation. The transcontinental railroad that linked East and West also led to the economic integration of the two regions. Before 1869, and in an era when the Panama Canal was not yet constructed, the West had been an isolated region where merchants had been able to charge higher prices and workers had been able to earn higher wages. The railroad changed that by permitting Eastern factories and merchants to compete directly with their West Coast counterparts. They no longer had to ship their merchandise on ships around the tip of South America to get to the Pacific Coast. Nor did they have to rely on slow overland transportation.

With their large centers of population, Eastern firms sold in large volume. They could manufacture items at less cost and sell at lower prices and still derive a substantial profit. As the Eastern firms shipped their goods across the continent on the railroad, Western merchants and factories had difficulty adjusting to this new situation. Faced with intense competition, employers lowered the wages for workers. Even that was oftentimes not enough as many Western factories succumbed to their Eastern rivals and closed down. Eventually, people in the West subscribed to the belief that their region was nothing more than "a colony" for Eastern firms and banks.

At the same time, the railroad permitted great numbers of European immigrants to move to the West. The latter period of the nineteenth century saw an enormous wave of immigration from Europe. Earlier generations of immigrants had largely settled along the Eastern seaboard of the United States. Many continued to do so. At the same time, however, railroads seeking passengers for their new routes were encouraging European

Anti-Chinese riot in Denver, Colorado, 1880. (Library of Congress)

immigrants to settle in the West. The arrival of these immigrants and other laborers who chose to move westward increased the competition for jobs. Wages predictably fell. Frustrated by the decline in their pay, laborers in the West sought scapegoats, and the Chinese were a convenient target. Depressions in the last three decades of the nineteenth century further exacerbated the situation.

The West Coast

Fueled by prejudice, competition, and economic change, a widespread anti-Chinese movement emerged on the West Coast and in the United States. It took the form of laws and statutes, immigration restrictions, exclusion, and violence such as riots and lynchings. The laws and statutes that were aimed at the Chinese were remarkably varied and detailed. The case of San Francisco and California may serve to illustrate this point, although other cities and states had similar examples.

In the 1870's, San Francisco passed a series of discriminatory ordinances to harass its Chinese population. The Cubic Air Ordinance required lodging houses to provide at least 500 cubic feet of air space for each person. Considering it to be an unfair law, the Chinese refused to pay the fine and went to jail. So many of them were there that the facility itself violated the ordinance.

This prompted the Board of Supervisors to pass a Queue Ordinance. The measure specified that male prisoners should have their hair cut to within one inch of their scalps. This meant that the Chinese would lose their queues or pigtails. This was a very severe punishment and could prevent their return to China, for Chinese without queues were viewed as rebels against the Ch'ing dynasty. After conquering China, the Manchus had decreed that Chinese male adults had to wear queues as a sign of their submission to foreign rule.

The Sidewalk Ordinance also singled out the Chinese. It said that people could not use sidewalks while carrying poles bearing goods. While the law seemed simple enough, it was really directed at the Chinese who balanced poles as a way of conveying loads. The ordinance was more of a nuisance, obstructing and impeding the Chinese in the conduct of their daily activities.

Since many Chinese were employed as laundrymen, it is not surprising that San Francisco passed a measure dealing with that occupation. The Laundry Ordinance required laundries employing a one-horse drawn vehicle to pay a license fee of two dollars quarterly, while those with two such vehicles paid four dollars quarterly. However, laundries that did not use any vehicles paid fifteen dollars quarterly. Since the Chinese were immigrants with less wealth and property, they fell into the last category. The ordinance was an example of regressive taxation, requiring more taxes from those who had less money.

As hostility towards the Chinese mounted in San Francisco, individuals were able to capitalize on that sentiment. Denis Kearney, a colorful sandlot orator, organized the Workingmen's Party in San Francisco in 1870 and molded it into a powerful political force. Although the Republican and Democratic parties in California already subscribed to anti-Chinese positions, Kearney was successful in capturing the public's attention by coining a slogan, "The Chinese Must Go!" As an independent third party, it rapidly established branches in Oakland, Sacramento, and Los Angeles.

In 1879, when California organized a convention to revise its state constitution, the Workingmen's Party was able to influence the outcome. Article Nineteen of the Second California Constitution dealt with the "Chinese or Mongolian" issue. Section Three stated that no corporation formed in California should employ Chinese under the penalty of a fine, or imprisonment, or both. Section Four said that Chinese were not to be employed by any unit of state, county, or municipal government, except as punishment for a crime.

In the discussions at the constitutional convention, the Chinese were repeatedly referred to as "Asiatics," "Coolies," and

Major Locations of Anti-Chinese Violence in the United States, 1870-1900

"Mongolians." Delegates described the Chinese as a vile and degraded breed, a despicable and inferior race. Some proposed anti-miscegenation legislation preventing the marriage of whites with Chinese. As a result, in the following year, the state's Civil Code was amended to prohibit the issuance of licenses permitting marriages between whites and Chinese.

At the same time, politicians and pressure groups in California attempted to discourage and to end Chinese immigration. As early as the 1850's, the state enacted taxes to collect revenue from the Chinese and those who gave them passage by ship. In 1858 California also passed a measure forbidding Chinese from entering the state. All such efforts were destined for failure, however, as the courts ruled that immigration policy was a matter reserved for the federal government.

Exclusion Achieved

This being the case, the arena shifted to the Congress and Washington. Congressmen and Senators from the Western states advocated passage of exclusion legislation against the Chinese in the 1870's. Southerners with a racial problem of their own joined with the Westerners, but there was also substantial support from Midwesterners and Easterners. Restriction of Chinese immigration had clearly become a national issue. In 1882 the U.S. Congress finally passed a Chinese Exclusion Act, which was signed by President Chester A. Arthur. The bill provided that the entry of Chinese laborers to the United States would be denied for ten years. Subsequent legislation in 1888, 1892, and 1902 tightened the restrictions and extended the exclusion policy. In 1904 and 1924, acts were passed which made exclusion permanent. Moreover, U.S. annexation of Hawaii in 1898 after the Spanish-American War soon extended the Chinese exclusion policy to the newly acquired island territory.

The Exclusion Act of 1882 was a humiliating episode for China. Never before had the United States excluded people from another country on the basis of ancestry or nationality. Up to this point, America had always maintained an open-door policy for immigration. But now that the policy had been breached, people from other lands could also be restricted or denied entry. In the future, the precedent of the Chinese Exclusion Act would have serious implications for immigration from Japan and Southern and Eastern Europe.

Even though the Exclusion Act of 1882 allowed Chinese other than laborers to enter the United States, a hostile Bureau of Immigration made entry difficult. Officials, merchants, students, teachers, and travelers, for example, who had the right to come to the United States were frequently subjected to rude treatment and arbitrary rejection by immigration inspectors. In 1905, angered by the callous and discriminatory treatment accorded their fellow countrymen, the public in China retaliated with a boycott against buying American goods. People in major cities such as Peking, Canton, and Shanghai all joined in the movement. Even overseas Chinese in Singapore, Canada, Japan, and the Philippines participated in the protest. As the first widespread and spontaneous expression of nationalism in China, it showed the indignation of the Chinese people everywhere, but the boycott ultimately was not successful.

Besides barring laborers, the Exclusion Act of 1882 also reaffirmed that first-generation Chinese could not be naturalized for American citizenship. This meant that Chinese immigrants, regardless of the length of their residence in the United States, could not be full-fledged Americans. Unable to vote and to participate in U.S. elections, they were legally isolated from the mainstream of American political life. As a result, they became acutely aware that their status was different from that of European immigrants who could be naturalized for American citizenship.

Victory for the exclusionists in 1882, however, did not curb the anti-Chinese movement. Violence and anger against the Chinese in the United States did not abate, but continued undiminished in a pattern already familiar along the mining frontier. In 1871, a bloody massacre took place in Los Angeles in which nearly a score of Chinese were killed by a mob. In 1882, in Rock Springs, Wyoming, another infamous episode occurred in which 28 Chinese were killed and 15 of them were wounded. The Chinese government vociferously protested the incident, and Congress agreed to pay an indemnity of over $147,000 for the damage done. In 1885 and 1886, mobs in Washington expelled the Chinese from Tacoma and tried to do the same in Seattle. In the following year at Snake River, Oregon, ten Chinese were murdered and robbed. Many other similar actions took place throughout the American West in the late nineteenth century as it became an open season for those opposed to the Chinese.

Chinese Resistance

Faced with this tide of anti-Chinese feeling, the Chinese did not remain passive. From the beginning of their settlement in the United States, they went to the courts and attempted to secure justice and fair treatment. But even this course was strewn with obstacles. For example, a person by the name of George Hall had killed a Chinese. He was tried and found guilty based upon the information supplied by Chinese witnesses, but when he appealed the decision in 1854, his conviction was thrown out. According to California statutes, blacks, mulattos, and American Indians could not testify against whites in court. As the Chinese were not whites, the California Supreme Court ruled that they were of another category and therefore could not give testimony against whites. This position was taken by the California courts until several years after the end of the Civil War, and it meant that the Chinese received no legal protection or redress against those who perpetrated acts aimed at them.

On the other hand, the Chinese also turned to the federal courts to resist racism and discriminatory treatment. There the record was somewhat mixed. Efforts to challenge the numerous exclusion acts and amendments passed since 1882 were generally to no avail. The U.S. Supreme Court ruled that Congress could enact legislation that might supersede previous international treaties or prior immigration policy. Some important victories, however, were also won. Ho Ah Kow, for example, contested the right of San Francisco to enforce its Queue Ordinance against him. In its 1879 decision, the U.S. Supreme Court ruled that the measure was discriminatory and violated the principle of equal protection granted in the Fourteenth Amendment of the Constitution. In 1886, the U.S. Supreme Court dealt a setback to San Francisco's laundry ordinances against the Chinese. In the case of *Yick Wo v. Hopkins*, the Justices ruled that laws which appeared to be neutral but were unfairly applied were discriminatory. They declared that citizens and aliens alike were entitled to the equal protection clause of the Fourteenth Amendment. Finally, in the case of Wong Kim Ark in 1898, the U.S. Supreme Court found in favor of a petition by an American-born Chinese. It ruled that, according to the Constitution, a person born in the United States was an American citizen, regardless of whether his parents were aliens or citizens.

For the anti-Chinese movement, the legislation passed in 1882 highlighted a major victory. Yet the reality remained that labor was still needed for the agriculture of the American West and Hawaii. Deprived of Chinese labor, employers and recruiters searched for alternative sources from Japan, Korea, India, the Philippines, and Mexico. In a cycle of ethnic succession, immigrants from all these countries would work in the fields. But in each case, although their labor would be valued, they would also elicit prejudice and discrimination as in the example of the Chinese.

6 Life Under Exclusion

Angel Island

Despite the breadth and the intensity of the anti-Chinese movement, many Chinese still sought admission to the United States. While the Exclusion Act of 1882 prevented laborers from entering, it did permit certain classes of people to come. Others seeking entry were Chinese who were American citizens by native birth or by derivation. Derivation referred to those who had acquired American citizenship through their parents or grandparents.

Although the Chinese could enter through several immigrant stations at different ports, the most important one for most of them was Angel Island in San Francisco Bay. Before 1910, most Chinese who immigrated to California were sent to a wooden shed on the wharf in San Francisco. But from 1910 to 1940, Angel Island became the "Ellis Island of the West." Newly arrived immigrants, mostly Chinese and other Asians, were sent there for processing, medical inspection, and interrogation. After a fire destroyed one of the buildings in the immigration station, the Angel Island facility was closed and immigrants were sent instead to San Francisco.

The label the "Ellis Island of the West" suggests the image of tired, huddling masses yearning to be free. Ellis Island in New York harbor, at the foot of the Statue of Liberty, offered European immigrants the promise of escape from difficult circumstances and the hope of a better life in America. To Chinese immigrants, however, Angel Island hardly represented the same radiant image. Located in San Francisco Bay near Alcatraz, a prison for notorious and hardened felons, Angel Island was seen as a barrier to thwart the entry of the Chinese.

Particularly after the passage of the Exclusion Act of 1882, immigration officials reflected hostile attitudes toward the Chinese. At the same time, many Chinese tried to gain admittance through claiming the status of "paper sons." They held papers purporting to be the sons of Chinese fathers with American citizenship, born during visits back to China. As a result, they had the legal right to immigrate to the United States. The catastrophic San Francisco earthquake and fire in 1906 destroyed many relevant documents and birth records, thereby opening the opportunity for false claims.

Suspicious and vigilant immigration officials tried to screen out the fraudulent paper sons by means of detailed questioning sessions. The Chinese, in turn, responded by producing crib sheets and "cram papers" to coach prospective immigrants about the correct answers to these inquiries. The tragedy was that legitimate immigrants might be refused admission due to a wrong answer or an honest failure to remember an insignificant fact. Moreover, individuals were confined for periods ranging from several weeks to several years while their medical status was examined and other aspects of their cases were reviewed. Consequently, for numerous Chinese, Angel Island became a symbol of prejudice and oppression, a legacy of living under the shadow of exclusion.

While detained at Angel Island, the Chinese wrote or carved poems on the walls registering their frustration, disappointment, and anger. Fearing deportation, many bemoaned their powerlessness and the uncertainty of their fate. One writer put it this way:

> America has power, but not justice.
> In prison, we were victimized as if we were
>   guilty.

Given no opportunity to explain, it was really
   brutal.
I bow my head in reflection but there is
   nothing I can do.

Angel Island immigration station in the 1920's. (National Archives)

Others lamented the economic circumstances that had led to their detention on Angel Island:

> This place is called an island of immortals,
> When, in fact, this mountain wilderness is a
>   prison.
> Once you see the open net, why throw
>   yourself in?
> It is only because of empty pockets I can do
>   nothing else.

Adapting to Exclusion

Those who were fortunate enough to be admitted to the United States found that most Chinese communities before World War II were predominantly male in composition. Several factors were responsible for this situation. First, many Chinese men who emigrated to the United States wanted their wives to remain in China, because they were not planning to establish permanent residence in the United States. Another factor was the Page Law, passed by the U.S. Congress in 1875. Ostensibly, this law was intended to prevent Chinese prostitutes from entering the country. In effect, however, the law barred Chinese women from entering the United States. Finally, the Exclusion Act of 1882, the Immigration Act of 1924, and various court decisions had a cumulative result of reducing the entry of Chinese women to an extremely small trickle.

As a result, Chinese communities were "bachelor societies," with imbalanced sex ratios heavily skewed towards male adults. There was a certain sadness to these communities, for in Chinese tradition, to be without family and children was tantamount to being a failure in life. In Chinatowns and other areas, Chinese bachelors and adult males lived together in boarding houses and fraternized in immigrant organizations and clubs.

Singled out by prejudice and discrimination and relegated to a marginal position in American society during this exclusionary era, the Chinese adapted to the situation in various ways. One response was to strengthen their ties to China. Many of the Chinese immigrants had arrived in the United States with a sojourning attitude. That is, they had hoped to make money in Gum Shan and then to return to live with family and relatives back in China. The unfriendly reception that they received convinced many that their original plans were correct, that America could never be a home to them. Focusing their attention on their ancestral regions and native villages, they dutifully sent remittances back to their families and kinfolk. They donated funds to set up schools and to build railroads and other public works. Thus, this flow of capital helped to spur economic development and the improvement of life in their home areas.

Periodically, many of the Chinese immigrants — if they had sufficient funds — might return to visit China. The regularization of shipping schedules across the Pacific Ocean made such forays back and forth much more feasible and convenient. Those who were fortunate enough to have married and started a family in the United States occasionally sent their children to attend schools and universities in China. The intent was to provide them with fluency in the Chinese language so that they could live in China or simply to maintain their cultural heritage. If such an option was not possible, children were sent to Chinese language schools established in the United States to learn about Chinese traditions and the Chinese language.

As they retired, some of the Chinese immigrants realized the dream of rejoining their families and friends in China. If they had been lucky and had prospered, they could reside comfortably in their home villages or neighborhoods. Others less successful also returned, while some were destined to remain in America, unable to amass funds to go back home.

Another response was to maintain an interest in the politics of China. This was especially so with the first-generation immigrants, who could not naturalize and become American citizens; they therefore could not vote in U.S. elections at the local, state, and national levels. But some of the Chinese holding

American citizenship also wanted to help China, for they hoped
to assist in the building of a modern China, free from poverty
and military weakness.

In the last decade of the nineteenth and the early part of the
twentieth centuries, Chinese reformers and revolutionaries hotly
debated the path for the modernization of China. Reformers, led
by individuals such as K'ang Yu-wei and Liang Ch'i-ch'ao,
favored the creation of a constitutional monarchy on the model of
Meiji Japan. Revolutionaries, on the other hand, led by Sun Yat-
sen, sought the overthrow of the imperial system, the liberation
of China from the Manchus, and the formation of a republic.
Attending Iolani School in Hawaii operated by the Anglican
Church of England, Sun received an education that taught him
about democracy and other Western ideas that could change
China. To the Empress dowager Tz'u-hsi, however, who ruled
China, the programs of both groups were unacceptable and she
viewed them as dangerous.

Nonetheless, the Chinese reformers and revolutionaries
continued to promote their ideas and sought support and money
from the overseas Chinese communities in Southeast Asia,
Japan, Hawaii, and North America. As they met with the
overseas Chinese in Hawaii and the United States, the two groups
competed for influence and followers. The reformers set up
Protect the Emperor societies to organize their supporters. In
opposition, the revolutionaries set up Revive China societies, later
renamed Revolutionary Alliance societies. Branches of the two
societies could be found in numerous cities throughout the United
States and Hawaii.

In 1911, a revolution finally took place in China and the
Manchu dynasty was toppled. In its stead, a Chinese republic
was formed, thus ushering in a phase of republican government
in China from 1911 to 1949. Unfortunately, without prior
experience, there was no consensus about how a republic should
operate. The Chinese republic was plunged into political chaos
and warlord rule until 1928. China was then unified by the
Kuomintang or the Nationalist party, the successor to the

Revolutionary Alliance. During the revolutionary and republican phases, Chinese from the United States played an important role. Some even returned to help modernize and to industrialize China.

═══════════════════════

The Second Generation

Amidst the changes taking place in China, it was easy to lose sight of equally significant trends occurring in the Chinese communities in America. With immigration from China virtually stopped and Chinese returning to their homeland, the Chinese population in the United States declined. At the same time, the percentage of American-born Chinese began to increase. After 1940, there were more American-born than foreign-born Chinese in the United States, a result of natural increase.

Unlike the first generation, this second generation held American citizenship and as adults could vote in U.S. elections. Attending American schools, they received a more intensive exposure to U.S. society than had been afforded their parents. Almost like windows to the larger society, they interpreted the dynamics of the outside to their parents, and they were a cultural bridge to the larger world beyond the Chinese community. This did not mean that they escaped prejudice and discrimination, however. Second-generation Chinese schoolchildren in San Francisco and Mississippi, for example, were subjected to school segregation just as blacks were. The immigrant Chinese parents were not necessarily at ease with their American-born offspring. Concerned about their children's command of the Chinese language and their understanding of Chinese culture, they often sent their sons and daughters to Chinese-language schools after the end of the regular school day. In these language schools, the American-born generation practiced calligraphy, studied Chinese geography and history, and learned about Confucian values and morality. Above all, they learned to communicate with the older generation, although in many cases the results of the schooling were varied at best.

As many of the American-born generation matured, they evidenced a Chinese American sensibility. To varying degrees, they were aware that in all likelihood they were going to live in the United States rather than in China. While retaining some aspects of their parents' culture, they also added elements from the culture of the host society. The result was a distinctive hybrid, Chinese American culture, which differed according to time and place for the American-born generation.

New organizations that catered to the second generation sprang up in the Chinese communities. One example was the Chinese American Citizens Alliance. Started in 1895, it was originally called the Native Sons of the Golden State. Membership was restricted to those Chinese who held American citizenship, and meetings were conducted in English. Renamed the Chinese American Citizens Alliance in 1915, the organization educated the Chinese in the United States about the importance of political participation and campaigned against politicians who were opposed to the Chinese. It maintained a newspaper, the *Chinese*

Three generations gather for this family portrait; exclusion had a cruel impact on Chinese American families. (Myrleen Ferguson/PhotoEdit)

Times, and established lodges or branches in cities such as San Francisco, Los Angeles, Fresno, Chicago, Boston, Pittsburgh, Detroit, and Portland.

While the majority of the second generation probably practiced Chinese popular religion, others converted to Christianity. In Chinese popular religion, Buddhism, Taoism, and Confucianism were fused together; it was often practiced in the privacy of the home rather than in a temple or shrine. On certain dates of the lunar calendar, various festivals and rituals were celebrated or observed, and there was a filial respect for deceased ancestors. A few Chinese immigrants had already converted to Christianity in China, but in the United States, larger numbers of the first- and second-generation Chinese became Christians. Chinese American Christian churches offered religion, social fellowship, and a chance to affiliate with other Chinese, all the benefits of immigrant churches in other ethnic communities.

The American-born Chinese also followed the currents and fads in American popular culture. They bought records and photographs, listened to the radio, went to the movies, and enjoyed music and dancing. In communities with large Chinese populations, musical groups, vaudeville acts, and night clubs provided entertainment. In San Francisco, for example, from the 1930's to the 1960's, a popular nightspot was the Chinese Forbidden City Night Club. Like the Cotton Club in New York's Harlem, which catered to blacks, Forbidden City catered to the Chinese and tourists in Chinatown. It featured chorus lines, cabaret scenes, tap dancing, and other colorful acts. In fact, it became the basis for Rodgers and Hammerstein's production of *Flower Drum Song*. In short, during the exclusionary era, the second generation and their parents were still socially and culturally isolated, but there was a yearning to belong and to participate fully in American society.

7 Changing Attitudes During Wartime and After

Repeal of Chinese Exclusion

World War II reshaped the modern world as most people know it, and it brought important changes to the status of the Chinese in the United States. Even though Americans see World War II as beginning on December 7, 1941, with the Japanese attack on Pearl Harbor in the Hawaiian Islands, the conflict had started much earlier for Europeans and Asians. In Europe, the war had begun in 1939 when Great Britain and France attempted to defend its ally Poland against an invasion by Nazi Germany. In Asia, the Pacific War may be said to have started in 1931 when Japan seized Manchuria from China or in 1937 when it tried to conquer the rest of China.

After the surprise attack at Pearl Harbor, the United States declared war against Japan. Now that China and the United States were allies against a common enemy, it became obvious to many that American exclusionary laws were an embarrassment in the war against the Axis Powers of Japan, Italy, and Germany. Why should people from a friendly country be treated as inferior or undesirable immigrants? A publisher, Richard Walsh, started a campaign to repeal the Chinese exclusion acts. Missionaries, businessmen, and others joined in the movement to end the

American policy of exclusion. A timely visit by Madame Chiang Kai-shek, the wife of the leader of the Chinese war effort against Japan, helped to bolster the campaign.

Within the Congress itself, the issue received serious debate. The supporters of veterans groups and patriotic societies, some labor interests, and southerners, opposed any changes regarding Chinese exclusion. They adhered to a narrower, more restrictive vision regarding the racial composition of America. On the other hand, religious organizations, businessmen, and others sympathetic to China, favored change. They argued that such a move would provide a boost to Chinese morale in the war against Japan. Also, as a practical measure, it would keep China in the war, forcing Japan to fight on several fronts. Moreover, fair treatment of China with respect to immigration would silence Japanese propaganda suggesting that the United States was discriminatory towards Asians. Finally, it was an ethical and moral thing to do, to end discrimination and make a statement

U.S. Navy recruiting station at the Chinese Consolidated Benevolent Association's headquarters in Los Angeles during World War II. (Library of Congress)

about racial equality. For his part, President Franklin Roosevelt supported the campaign to end exclusion.

As a result, in 1943, the U.S. Congress repealed the Chinese exclusion laws and offered new legislation. Chinese were granted an annual quota for 105 "persons of the Chinese race" to come to America. In addition, Chinese of the first generation, who had been born abroad, were eligible for naturalization to receive American citizenship. In some ways, the new policy was still marked by discrimination. The quota was clearly a token amount. Moreover, the term "persons of the Chinese race" indicated that any person of Chinese descent or ancestry from countries other than China were to be charged against the quota. This was not the usual practice, for immigrants from other nations were normally tallied against a "country of birth" formula. Nevertheless, China and the Chinese in the United States were generally happy about the measure. First-generation Chinese qualified for American citizenship, and many stepped forward to take advantage of the naturalization provision.

Other Related Legislation Key Changes

As the United States mobilized for war against the Axis Powers, Chinese Americans contributed significantly to the effort. As early as the 1930's, the Chinese in America had launched "Bowl of Rice" campaigns for humanitarian relief in war-torn China. The theme was that people should forego one bowl of rice and donate the proceeds to help the victims of war in China. After the United States joined the war, the Chinese staged rallies to encourage people to buy war bonds or to donate to the Red Cross. Others enlisted to fight in the armed forces, and many saw service in the China-Burma-India theater in the Pacific. After the war, some also served in the U.S. occupation of Japan or were stationed in South Korea.

At the end of the war, Congress passed other legislation that benefited Chinese Americans. A sympathetic Congress felt that

American men and women in uniform had served heroically on the front lines to defend the United States and to achieve victory. The War Brides Act in 1945 and the Fiancees Act in 1946 were passed to expedite entry by alien brides and fiancees. Chinese Americans were therefore able to bring Chinese women into the United States.

Because of the political chaos and economic difficulty of the many countries shattered by war, the Congress passed a Displaced Persons Act in 1948. This piece of legislation followed an earlier Presidential directive of 1945 in giving admittance to displaced persons. Later versions of this act allowed Chinese refugees to enter the United States.

In the postwar climate, there was considerable pressure to extend immigration quotas to other Asians as had occurred for the Chinese in 1943. Consequently, in 1952, Congress passed the McCarran-Walter Act, which allotted racial quotas to Asian countries in a designated Asia-Pacific triangle. The act also allowed Asians to undergo naturalization and race was no longer a bar to American citizenship. Thus, Japan was accorded a quota, and first-generation Japanese immigrants were able to achieve U.S. citizenship.

Reviewing the changes introduced during World War II and its aftermath, it is clear that the consequences were momentous for the Chinese in the United States. Not only was an immigration quota granted, but the naturalization of the first generation was also achieved. Moreover, the war caused a shortage of labor on the home front. Chinese Americans were hired in war industries and defense plants and escaped the confines of Chinatowns. In addition, those who had served in the armed forces benefited from the G.I. Bill that allowed veterans to get a subsidized college education with the help of the U.S. government.

The expansion of the postwar economy enabled many Chinese to enter the middle class. Those who held college degrees or had advanced training were able to become white-collar professionals. Job opportunities opened up in relative abundance, a great contrast to the prewar era. The legislative acts of 1943, 1952, and other bills permitted stranded wives and families in China to join Chinese in the United States. New immigrants helped to lessen somewhat the disproportionate ratio of male to female adults, and new families were started. Finally, a Confession Program begun by the U.S. government offered those who had entered the country illegally an opportunity to confess and to gain legal status.

The Cold War and Fear of Communism

While legal barriers against the Chinese were beginning to fall and prejudice was starting to recede, other problems arose. The fear of Communism and the rise of the Cold War cast a pall over the Chinese in the United States. At the end of World War II, a bitter civil war took place in China between the Nationalists and the Communists. By 1949, the Communists had emerged victorious and had established the People's Republic of China with its capital in Beijing. The Nationalists fled to the island of Taiwan, where they maintained a government in exile for the Republic of China, hoping for an eventual return to the Chinese mainland. To some concerned Americans, the "loss of China" gave the Soviet Union an advantage in its Cold War rivalry with the United States. Such fears were fueled by the Communist North Korean invasion of South Korea in 1950, with subsequent participation by the Chinese Communists. Partly due to the Korean War, the United States continued to recognize the Republic of China on Taiwan and did not extend diplomatic recognition to Communist China for nearly thirty years.

In the United States, public fears about Communism led to the development of McCarthyism. A U.S. Senator from Wisconsin, Joseph McCarthy, publicized the danger of Communist subversion. Because of the Communist triumph on mainland China and its entry into the Korean War in 1950, Chinese in America knew that they were prime suspects for being Communist agents. Existing prejudice merged with hysteria to wreak havoc among Chinese Americans. The McCarran-Walter Act of 1952, for example, contained an internal security provision that authorized the creation of camps to house subversives. Already familiar with the internment camps in which Japanese Americans were imprisoned from 1942 to 1945, some Chinese Americans thought that they might suffer the same fate. In operating the Confession Program, the Immigration and Naturalization Service launched raids on Chinese communities in 1956. The alleged purpose was to net those who had entered the United States under fraudulent means, but another goal was to arrest those who held unpopular views or were sympathetic to mainland China.

The Federal Bureau of Investigation encouraged people living in Chinatowns to become informants to turn in Communist subversives. Partisans who sided with the Nationalists on Taiwan found it a convenient opportunity to harass their critics, who were not necessarily Communists. Individuals with personal feuds or disputes discovered a means to get even. The motion picture industry in Hollywood also fed the hysteria by producing a film entitled *Cripple Creek* in 1952. In the movie, Chinese in a laundry secretly plot to send gold back to Communist China from the United States. In short, the 1950's were a decade during which Chinese Americans had to reckon with heightened governmental surveillance of their activities.

Statehood for Hawaii

The fear of Communism even tainted the prospect of statehood for Hawaii in 1959. As an island territory in the Pacific, Hawaii was a pluralistic society with many different ethnic groups such as Hawaiians, Caucasians, Japanese, Chinese, Filipinos, Koreans, and Puerto Ricans. No single group constituted a majority, and every group was a minority. But because Caucasians were a minority and nonwhite peoples collectively were a majority, some American southerners expressed reservations about the desirability of the Hawaii's fitness for statehood.

Furthermore, in the climate of the 1950's, the large number of Asians in Hawaii's population raised questions about the presence of Communist subversives. Mainland China had turned Communist, North Korea was Communist, Communist Huk rebels were troubling the Philippines, and left-wing Marxist organizations were known to be active in Japan. The territory seemed to have sympathy for the Democratic party, but the Democrats included longshoremen, union members, and others who subscribed to liberal or left of center sentiments. Finally, Hawaii was a small territory with a small population and a small economy and was not contiguous to the lower 48 states in North America.

Quite fortuitously, however, a number of factors worked on behalf of Hawaiian statehood. First, Alaska had preceded Hawaii in becoming the 49th state. It had an even smaller population, was perceived to have a weaker "icebox" economy, and was also not connected directly to the lower 48 states. Second, many tourists and military personnel who had served in the Pacific cherished fond memories of the islands. Finally, there was bipartisan cooperation for the cause of Hawaiian statehood. Two influential southern Democrats, Speaker Sam Rayburn of the House of Representatives and Majority Leader Lyndon Johnson of the Senate, favored statehood for Hawaii. Likewise, the popular military hero of World War II and Republican president Dwight Eisenhower endorsed the idea of Hawaiian statehood. For all these reasons, Hawaii with its diverse mix of peoples, a large number of whom were Chinese, became the 50th state of the United States.

As the newest state in the union, the "Aloha State" became an important role model for Asian Americans in the other 49 states. On the basis of their ability and popularity, Americans of Asian ancestry rose to prominent posts or high political positions. Thus, Daniel Inouye was elected to the U.S. House of Representatives in 1959 and, in 1962, became the first Japanese American to serve in the U.S. Senate. In 1974, George Ariyoshi, a Japanese American, became the first Asian American to win office as the

A Taiwanese musician at a New York summer festival; many post-1965 Chinese immigrants have come from Taiwan. (Robert Brenner/PhotoEdit)

governor of a state. And a second-generation Chinese American, Hiram Fong, became the first Chinese American and the first Asian American to serve in the U.S. Senate, in 1959.

Immigration Act of 1965

A few years later, a pivotal milestone occurred in the form of the Immigration Act of 1965. Signed by President Lyndon Johnson, the measure introduced key changes in immigration to America. From the Western Hemisphere, the bill permitted a total of 120,000 immigrants per year, without any per-country limitation. From the Eastern Hemisphere, 170,000 persons could be admitted annually, with a limit of 20,000 from any single country. The larger quota assigned to the Eastern Hemisphere was intended to alleviate the great desire to immigrate to the

United States, a situation that had been aggravated by the small numbers permitted in the McCarran-Walter Act of 1952. Furthermore, the legislation was seen as a means of fostering family reunification and redressing the unfairness of previous immigration legislation. Finally, the bill was heralded as an indication that the United States welcomed immigrants from both the East and the West. Affixing his signature to the legislation at Ellis Island near the foot of the Statue of Liberty, President Johnson made a dramatic statement about the goal to end discrimination and prejudice in U.S. immigration policy.

For the Chinese in the United States, the Immigration Act of 1965 was a welcomed event. Family members and relatives no longer had to endure long waiting lists resulting from the small quota conceded in McCarran-Walter Act. As more Chinese arrived in America, changes began to take place. By 1980, the U.S. census showed that the percentage of foreign-born Chinese was greater than that of the American-born Chinese. This reversal from the period following the 1940's was merely a reflection of the small numbers of Chinese in the U.S. after the enactment of the exclusionary laws of the 1880's. Old Chinatowns experienced new growth and vitality, even as other Chinese moved outward to the suburbs and away from the West Coast.

Additional legislation in 1986 and 1990 increased the rate of emigration from the British colony of Hong Kong. Diplomatic recognition of the People's Republic of China in 1979 by the United States allowed renewed immigration from mainland China. At the same time, America maintained informal ties with the Republic of China on Taiwan, and the people of the island nation were also given a quota. In retrospect, then, the period of World War II and its aftermath had led to crucial legislation that significantly affected the fate of the Chinese community in America.

Chinese Population in the U.S.

State	Population	% of Total U.S. Chinese Population
Alabama	3,929	.2%
Alaska	1,342	.1%
Arizona	14,136	.9%
Arkansas	1,726	.1%
California	704,850	42.8%
Colorado	8,659	.5%
Connecticut	11,082	.7%
Delaware	2,301	.1%
District of Columbia	3,144	.2%
Florida	30,737	1.9%
Georgia	12,657	.8%
Hawaii	68,804	4.2%
Idaho	1,420	.1%
Illinois	49,936	3.0%
Indiana	7,371	.4%
Iowa	4,442	.3%
Kansas	5,330	.3%
Kentucky	2,736	.2%
Louisiana	5,430	.3%
Maine	1,262	.1%
Maryland	30,868	1.9%
Massachusetts	53,792	3.3%
Michigan	19,145	1.2%
Minnesota	8,980	.5%
Mississippi	2,518	.2%
Missouri	8,614	.5%
Montana	655	.0%
Nebraska	1,775	.1%
Nevada	6,618	.4%
New Hampshire	2,314	.1%
New Jersey	59,084	3.6%
New Mexico	2,607	.2%
New York	284,144	17.3%
North Carolina	8,859	.5%
North Dakota	557	.0%
Ohio	19,447	1.2%
Oklahoma	5,193	.3%
Oregon	13,652	.8%
Pennsylvania	29,562	1.8%
Rhode Island	3,170	.2%
South Carolina	3,039	.2%
South Dakota	385	.0%
Tennessee	5,653	.3%
Texas	63,232	3.8%
Utah	5,322	.3%
Vermont	679	.0%
Virginia	21,238	1.3%
Washington	33,962	2.1%
West Virginia	1,170	.1%
Wisconsin	7,354	.4%
Wyoming	554	.0%
TOTAL	1,645,472	

SOURCE: U.S. Census Bureau, 1990 Census.

8 Contemporary Life

Demographic Changes and Diversity

"San Francisco is the center of Chinese America." Before World War II, that was the perception of many Chinese in the United States. Since the passage of the Immigration Act of 1965, however, that statement is less true. The influx of new Chinese immigrants and a greater openness in American society has led to new demographic trends and different societal patterns. While many Chinese continue to reside in California, many others have settled in states in the Midwest, the East, and the South. New York is now in second place. And although Hawaii is in third place, it is followed by Texas, New Jersey, Massachusetts, and Illinois. The second tier is headed by Washington, followed by Maryland, Florida, Pennsylvania, Virginia, Ohio, and Michigan.

Even as the older Chinatowns have received a breath of new life from the incoming immigrants, other Chinese communities have arisen in the suburbs and other locales. Moreover, many Chinese no longer feel constrained to live with other Chinese, and they have dispersed throughout the United States. As societal attitudes have changed and the laws against intermarriage have fallen by the wayside, many Chinese have married into other racial and ethnic groups. Among all the different states, Hawaii has one of the highest rates of outmarriage for Chinese Americans. Before the 1960's, the lingua franca or dominant dialects for the Chinese communities in San Francisco and Honolulu were the Toishan and Chungshan dialects, respectively, two variants of Cantonese. But the recent immigration legislation has led to the arrival of many Chinese from Taiwan, mainland

China, Hong Kong, and Southeast Asia. In addition, the end of the Vietnam and Southeast Asian conflict led to large numbers of Chinese refugees from Laos, Vietnam, and Cambodia. Chinese in the United States today speak a variety of different dialects, ranging from several versions of Cantonese and Fukienese to Mandarin.

Diverse backgrounds and different dialects have also resulted in establishment of new organizations. The new immigrants feel that traditional societies do not cater to their needs as well, so they have created their own. Consequently, associations serving Chinese from Taiwan, mainland China, and Vietnam or Southeast Asia have been started. Professionals finding it helpful to affiliate with others in the same occupation have set up alternative organizations. Christian churches and Buddhist temples or monasteries have been opened to give the new arrivals the support and religion that they desire. And to keep the children knowledgeable about their language and cultural heritage,

Chinatown in Washington, D. C.; while Chinese Americans continue to reside in California and Hawaii, many have settled on the East Coast and elsewhere throughout the United States. (Susan Hormuth)

language schools teaching Cantonese and Mandarin have appeared.

The politics of foreign policy has also become much more complex and divisive. In 1979, the United States decided to recognize mainland China and established formal diplomatic relations with the People's Republic of China. Embassies and consulates were set up between the two countries. The Republic of China on Taiwan was no longer recognized diplomatically by the U.S., and it suddenly became a legal nonentity in American foreign relations. Nevertheless, because of strategic interest and economic relations, informal ties were maintained between the United States and Taiwan. Among the Chinese in America, there are those who are supporters of mainland China or Taiwan. At the same time, there are others who advocate an independent Republic of Taiwan, a view that is not welcomed by either the People's Republic of China or the Republic of China. Most Chinese Americans, however, have chosen to stay neutral on the issue of the two Chinas.

Chinatown in Los Angeles. (Phil Borden/PhotoEdit)

The Model Minority Image

Just as the Chinese American population was registering rapid growth in the 1960's and 1970's, the national media in the United States began to speak about Chinese Americans and Asian Americans as a "Model Minority." In the midst of the civil rights movement and the Vietnam War era, Asian Americans were extolled as a model minority: quiet, industrious, and successful. They were members of the middle class that others would do well to imitate. Despite cultural differences and prejudice, they had been able to realize the American dream.

For Chinese American activists, this image was not received with enthusiasm. First, in the context of the period, the hidden message seemed to be that blacks, Hispanics, Native Americans, and other groups should alter their mindsets and adopt the behavior of Chinese Americans. But some Chinese in the United States had no wish to be a political football between other ethnic minorities and the larger society. They felt that the circumstances faced by other groups were different from those of Chinese Americans. In any event, they believed that American society should embark upon a "Second Reconstruction" to improve the civil rights and the social and economic status of all groups. The experience of Chinese Americans should not be used to distract the attention of the larger society from pursuing this agenda.

Secondly, the model minority image disguised the real history of the Chinese in the United States. The climb into middle-class status had been a long and arduous one. Prejudice and discrimination had colored the first century of the Chinese presence in America. Exclusion had reduced the size of the Chinese population and placed the first generation in a marginal, outcaste status. Only when the United States and China were together at war against Japan did the situation improve. Furthermore, a more liberalized and generous immigration policy for the Chinese did not occur until the 1960's. Even the legal barriers against intermarriage in many states did not fall until the civil rights laws of the 1960's.

Third, the model minority image falsely suggested that Chinese Americans were free from social and economic problems. Nothing could be further from the truth. Analyses of census figures indicate that the Chinese population in the United States is a bimodal one. Many have middle-class status, but a large number are also of the lower class and are marked by poverty. The fact that most Chinese Americans live in areas where the cost of living is high only compounds the problem. Last, because more members of Chinese families work than in the average American family, the per family income seems high, but the per capita breakdown is lower.

Chinese American communities actually have encountered serious growing pains since the 1960's. Rapid acculturation, urban poverty, rising expectations, and inattention to children due to working parents have contributed to the rise of juvenile delinquency and gang activity. Increased numbers of elderly population, immigrants with limited English proficiency, a lack of affordable housing, and unemployment are some of the issues that need to be faced. In addition, job discrimination with the problem of a "glass ceiling" and anti-Asian violence are other concerns. Chinese American activists and social workers have attempted to meet with government agencies and officials to solve these problems.

In trying to gain the attention of government officials and social agencies, Chinese Americans have discovered that community organization and political participation are extremely important. Whether in relation to civil rights issues or social concerns, the education of Chinese Americans and the mobilization of voters is necessary. Consequently, older organizations such as the Chinese American Citizens Alliance and the Chinese Consolidated Benevolent Association and newer ones such as the Organization of Chinese Americans, Self Help for the Elderly, and Chinese for Affirmative Action have emphasized the significance of political action.

On occasion, Chinese Americans have resorted to litigation to secure legal remedies. One such instance was the famous *Lau v.*

Nichols case in 1974. A group of Chinese American parents in San Francisco felt that the school district was not responsive to the limited English fluency of their children. They believed that the education of their children was being compromised. Accordingly, they took legal action against the school district; ultimately, the case was heard by the U.S. Supreme Court. In a landmark decision, the Court ruled that the San Francisco School District had an obligation to provide a meaningful education for its students. Some means had to be found to help immigrant children learn the material in their classes. This decision laid the legal basis for bilingual education in the United States.

Finally, some Chinese Americans attack the model minority image because they see it as a stereotype. In the past, the Chinese have had to contend with negative stereotypes, as personified by Sax Rohmer's fictional character Fu Manchu, a criminal mastermind who possesses many of the qualities traditionally ascribed to "Orientals": cunning, cruelty, inscrutability, knowledge of strange lore. Yet so-called positive stereotypes can be just as insidious and harmful. Thus, many Chinese Americans dislike Earl Derr Biggers' Charlie Chan character, the hero of a popular series of novels and movies in the 1920's, 1930's, and 1940's. While Chan is a shrewd and benevolent detective, he is depicted as talking as if he had sprung out of a fortune cookie. Such portrayals foster the perception that Chinese Americans are always aliens, perpetual strangers and foreigners, and forever inscrutable.

The model minority image at the student level portrays Chinese Americans as being bookish and academic drones. They are supposed to be scholastic eggheads with narrow interests confined to educational topics. This type of a stereotype proved to be detrimental recently, when it was learned that Ivy League and other selective universities had deliberately imposed quotas on the admission of Chinese Americans. This was reminiscent of the quotas imposed upon the admission of Jews to institutions of higher learning several decades earlier. In this case, however, the excuse used by the universities was that the extracurricular

States with Highest Chinese American Populations

1.	California	704,850	42.8%
2.	New York	284,144	17.3%
3.	Hawaii	68,804	4.2%
4.	Texas	63,232	3.8%
5.	New Jersey	59,084	3.6%
6.	Massachusetts	53,792	3.3%
7.	Illinois	49,936	3.0%
8.	Washington	33,962	2.1%
9.	Maryland	30,868	1.9%
10.	Florida	30,737	1.9%
11.	Pennsylvania	29,562	1.8%
12.	Virginia	21,238	1.3%
13.	Ohio	19,447	1.2%
14.	Michigan	19,145	1.2%
15.	Arizona	14,136	.9%

records of Chinese Americans were deficient and that no quota system existed anyway. Studies show, though, that the extracurricular activities of Chinese Americans are no less diverse than those of other students. And, under probing by the Justice Department and the Office of Civil Rights, many universities have abandoned their admission quotas for Asian Americans and Chinese Americans.

Objections to the model minority image notwithstanding, Chinese Americans do take pride in the accomplishments and successes achieved by their community. Chinese American students have excelled in their studies at the school and university level, and they have received national recognition for their achievements. Chinese American scientists and educators have pioneered on the frontiers of research and have won international renown for their discoveries, while Chinese American entrepreneurs and professionals have made important contributions to the U.S. economy and society.

Breaking Stereotypes

Chinese American writers and artists have done much to expand awareness on the part of the larger society regarding the diversity and creativity of the Chinese American community. They have helped to destroy stereotypes about Chinese Americans as a monolithic and homogeneous group. At the same time, they have provided audiences with fresh and exciting forms of literary and cultural expression.

Frank Chin, a playwright and a writer, is one individual who has challenged conventional understandings about Chinese Americans. In his plays *The Chickencoop Chinaman* (1972) and *Year of the Dragon* (1975), he penetrates beneath the tourist veneer that cloaks Chinatowns and the lives of Chinese Americans. In an anthology iconoclastically entitled *Aiiieeeee!* (1975), he and his coauthors sought to give voice to Asian Americans who were born in the United States. Chin has been extremely critical of some of the best-known Chinese-American writers — another reminder to the larger society that many different viewpoints are represented within the Chinese-American community.

David Henry Hwang, a playwright, has written *FOB* (1979) and *M. Butterfly* (1988). In *FOB*, he explores the contrasting viewpoints of the immigrant, "Fresh Off the Boat," versus that of the ABC or "American-born Chinese," and tries to bring about a reconciliation from the mistrust that the two have for each other. In *M. Butterfly* Hwang parodies Eurocentrism and Western stereotypes about the exotic, "mystic East." Through the plays of Frank Chin, David Henry Hwang, Genny Lim, and others, flourishing theater groups such as the East West Players and the Asian American Theater Workshop have been established to train actors and to portray realistically the life experiences of Asian Americans.

Writers such as Lawrence Yep, Amy Tan, and Eleanor Wong Telemaque have also expanded the cultural landscape for Chinese

Chinese Americans are working together with other Asian Americans on a wide variety of economic and cultural programs. (Phil Borden/PhotoEdit)

Americans. In children's books such as *Dragonwings* (1975), *Sweetwater* (1976), and *Child of the Owl* (1977), Yep delves with great sensitivity into the themes of identity and interethnic relationships. In *The Joy Luck Club* (1989), Tan traces the bonds among mothers and their daughters. And in *It's Crazy to Stay Chinese in Minnesota* (1978), Telemaque wrestles with the question of what it means to be Chinese in a small town with few Chinese residents.

Filmmakers such as Wayne Wang and Felicia Lowe use a different medium to portray Chinese Americans. In films such as *Chan is Missing* (1981), *Dim Sum* (1987), and *Eat a Bowl of Tea* (1989), Wang reveals different aspects of the Chinese American reality, ranging from the cultural complexities of a Chinatown community, to the intimate ties between a mother and a daughter, to life in a bachelor society. Lowe, on the other hand, prefers to

produce documentaries; in *Carved in Silence* (1988), she retraces
the Chinese encounter with the Angel Island immigration station
in San Francisco Bay.

In short, through their talent and imagination, artists and
writers have helped to reshape thinking about Chinese
Americans. In the process, they have fostered an appreciation for
the contributions of Chinese Americans and have furthered the
vision of a richly multicultural America living in ethnic harmony.
As the Chinese American poet Wing Tek Lum, who lives in
Hawaii, so aptly put in his poem "Chinese Hot Pot":

> My dream of America
> is like da bin louh
> with people of all persuasions and tastes
> sitting down around a common pot
> chopsticks and basket scoops here and there
> some cooking squid and others beef
> some tofu or watercress
> all in one broth
> like a stew that really isn't
> as each one chooses what he wishes to eat
> only that the pot and the fire are shared
> along with the good company
> and the sweet soup
> spooned out at the end of the meal.

9 Some Who Made a Difference

Since the first arrival of the Chinese in the United States, there have been those who have made a difference in the life of the community. Often braving adverse public opinion and willing to incur risks, they have fought for the rights of Chinese Americans. Whether succeeding or failing in their efforts or personal accomplishments, they were pioneers who opened the doors to equality and freedom of cultural expression in the United States. In this sense, they were trailblazers who deserve to be remembered in any history of Chinese Americans.

Joseph and Mary Tape

Education is highly valued among Chinese Americans, so it is not surprising that many cases of litigation have focused on this issue. San Francisco had segregated its Chinese schoolchildren from 1859 until 1871, when it refused to fund any more classes for them. Chinese parents then had to hire private teachers or send their youth to church-sponsored schools. In 1884, Joseph and Mary Tape decided to challenge this practice by enrolling their daughter Mamie in Spring Valley School. Because the district superintendent had told the school principal Jennie Hurley to deny admission, the Tapes filed suit in court. The case of *Tape v. Hurley* was appealed to the Supreme Court of California, but the justices unanimously sustained the lower court decision of Judge James Maguire. Children born of Chinese parents in California had a right to a public education. In response, the San Francisco School District set up a separate Chinese Primary School in 1885. It later became the Oriental School and in 1924 was renamed the Commodore Stockton School.

In Mississippi, Gong Lum tried to have his daughter retained in a Rosedale high school for whites. His challenge, however, was destined to be unsuccessful. In the case of *Gong Lum v. Rice* in 1927, the state's Supreme Court ruled that Martha Lum could be segregated into a black school, based on the 1890 Mississippi Constitution which provided for separate educational facilities for non-whites. Thus, the decision followed the reasoning behind the "separate but equal" principle established by the U.S. Supreme Court in its *Plessy v. Ferguson* decision in 1896.

Yum Sinn Chang

A somewhat different episode regarding education occurred in Hawaii. The outstanding Chinese language school in the state is Mun Lun School, founded in 1911 and still operating today. In the mid-1930's, with more than 1,300 students, it was the largest Chinese educational institution in the United States. For much of its history, its guiding leader was Yum Sinn Chang. Originally recruited from the Tai Tung Chinese School in Yokohama, Japan, to teach in 1911, he became principal of Mun Lun School in 1915.

During his tenure as principal, a period of more than fifty years, Chang had to defend the school against severe attacks. For example, in 1921, the territorial legislature of Hawaii passed a Foreign Language School Bill. The measure levied an annual fee of one dollar per foreign language student and restricted classes to not more than an hour each day. Moreover, all foreign language school teachers were required to pass an examination in English, American history, and the Constitution of the United

States. After three years, however, the issue was taken to the courts, and the bill was declared unconstitutional. All the fees that had been collected were ordered refunded to the language schools.

After the Japanese attack on Pearl Harbor, all foreign language schools in the Hawaiian islands were closed by military decree. Even after martial law ended there in 1944, the restrictions were maintained. Emphasizing Americanism, the territorial legislature had passed a bill against the opening of the language schools. American children of Chinese ancestry were deprived of the opportunity to study Chinese language and culture. Finally, Yum Sinn Chang and a group of concerned individuals from the Chinese community decided to contest the validity of the legislation in court. In 1948 a decision came forth and the language school law was ruled unconstitutional. Chinese language schools such as Mun Lun School were able to operate once again. Highly respected as an educator, Chang continued to serve as principal until 1966. Many of the leaders of the Chinese community in Hawaii have been his former pupils.

Chang-Lin Tien

Although Chinese Americans have excelled in university teaching and research, none had headed a major research university. That situation changed in 1990, however, as Chang-lin Tien was selected the chancellor of the University of California at Berkeley. He therefore presides over one of the premier institutions of higher education in the United States and one that is internationally renowned for its pathbreaking research and instruction. By virtue of his position, Tien is a key spokesman for American educational policy and the Chinese American community.

Born in China, Tien completed his undergraduate education at National Taiwan University. Continuing his education, he received an M.A. at the University of Louisville and then an

M.A. and Ph.D. at Princeton University. A fine engineer, he soon became known for his research work in the field of heat transfer technology. But he was also a talented instructor, and in 1962, at age twenty-six, he was the youngest professor to win the Distinguished Teaching Award at the University of California. In his brilliant career, he has already earned many national and international honors. In the Chinese American community, he has helped many worthwhile causes. At the same time, he has strongly advocated the belief that higher education in America must be more responsive to the needs of its diverse student population.

Ng Poon Chew

Journalism is an important means to educate people and to inform the public. Ng Poon Chew was a Presbyterian minister who was a graduate of the San Francisco Theological Seminary. Feeling that newspapers could play a pivotal role in the Chinese community, he started the *Wah Mei Sun Bo* (*Chinese American Morning Paper*) in Los Angeles in 1898. Two years later, he moved north to San Francisco and published the *Chung Sai Yat Bo* (*Chinese Western Daily*). A progressive reformer and an educator, his paper supported republicanism, modernization, and reform for China. Its editorials and news articles criticized old customs and even championed equal rights for women. Socially polished and a fluent speaker of English, he was often asked to address non-Chinese audiences. In speaking to these groups, he promoted good relations between China and the United States and intercultural understanding. Aware of the plight of his fellow Chinese in California, he criticized the harmful aspects of America's exclusionary and discriminatory laws. By the time of his death in 1931, he had received numerous accolades and honors.

Hung Wai Ching

It takes a special kind of courage and compassion to cross ethnic boundaries and befriend a pariah group during wartime. Hung Wai Ching, a YMCA secretary in Honolulu, demonstrated that kind of exemplary heroism during World War II. Even before Pearl Harbor, he had helped form a Committee for Inter-Racial Unity in Hawaii to foster harmony among the different groups in the event of war with Japan. After December 7, 1941, Ching's trust and confidence in the loyalty of Hawaii's Japanese never wavered. He believed that their hearts were with America and that they were not a menace. He repeatedly seized opportunities to speak out on their behalf.

When second-generation Japanese Americans, called Nisei, were crestfallen because they had been discharged from the military, Ching urged them to fight for the right to serve their country. This determination became the basis for the 100th Battalion and the 442nd Regimental Combat Team, which were made up of Nisei. As these young Japanese Americans volunteered for military service and were selected to be trained on the U.S. mainland, Ching went along to pave the way. He traveled to the training sites and met with people to allay the fears of residents in the adjacent communities. After the war, he also helped in the adjustment of many of the returning veterans by helping them to find jobs and scholarships. In 1985, the Japanese American community celebrated the 100th anniversary of Japanese immigration to Hawaii. In its commemorative ceremonies, community leaders cited Hung Wai Ching as one to whom they owed *kansha* or enduring gratitude and appreciation.

Loni Ding

Another Chinese American, Loni Ding, has recently been lauded for her poignant films about the military experience of

Japanese Americans. Having once pursued advanced graduate studies, she decided to embark upon a career in filmmaking. After producing films such as *Bean Sprouts* and *How We Got Here*, about Chinese Americans, she turned her attention to Japanese Americans. In *Color of Honor: The Japanese American Soldier in World War II*, she crafted a film about those in the Military Intelligence Service who served in the Pacific theater. In a subsequent work, *Nisei Soldier: Standard Bearer for an Exiled People*, she traced the exploits of the highly decorated 442nd Regimental Combat Team that fought in Europe, even as 120,000 Japanese in the United States were imprisoned in internment camps. The filmmaker is now focusing her interests on documenting other aspects of the Asian American experience.

Hiram L. Fong

Politics is a way of getting representation and influencing public policy. It is also the vital process that keeps government democratic and close to the people. For Hiram L. Fong, it would be a remarkable climb to be elected as the first Asian American and the first Chinese American to sit in the United States Senate. Born the son of immigrants from China who worked on a plantation in Hawaii, Fong persevered against great odds. He attended McKinley High School in downtown Honolulu, nicknamed "Tokyo High" because of its large mix of immigrant children. After graduation, he worked and went to the University of Hawaii. Then he continued on to Harvard Law School.

After receiving his law degree, Fong returned to Hawaii, entered the bar, and started a highly successful law practice and business. Early in his career, he also affiliated with the Republican party and served in the territorial legislature. When Hawaii achieved statehood in 1959, its voters selected him as one of its two U.S. Senators. In the nation's capital, he carved out a role for himself as a "citizen of the Pacific" and strove to remove barriers against Asian immigration. He cooperated with President

Hiram L. Fong (Library of Congress)

Lyndon Johnson in the passage of the Immigration Act of 1965, which eliminated the severe restrictions on Asian immigration. Winning reelection twice, Fong earned a reputation as an expert on Asian and Pacific affairs who tried to strengthen goodwill and understanding between East and West.

Maxine Hong Kingston

Few writers have captured the epic of the Chinese American experience as boldly and as imaginatively as Maxine Hong Kingston. A second-generation Chinese American, she was born and raised in Stockton, California, where her immigrant parents ran a laundry business. A graduate of the University of California at Berkeley, Kingston writes to reclaim the history of the Chinese in America through literature. In two books of rare distinction, *The Woman Warrior* (1976) and *China Men* (1980), she surveyed with artistry and subtlety the drama of the Chinese American past. The public can readily identify with the hopes and the disappointments, the yearning and the pain, of Chinese immigrants and their descendants in America.

Beyond their significance for Chinese Americans, her works have broad appeal for others as well. A modest person by nature, Maxine Hong Kingston is a writer of quiet conviction and philosophical integrity. She unflinchingly supports issues of social justice and humanitarian concern. Readers of *The Woman Warrior* and *China Men* can see her treatment of universal themes about humanity and the indomitable human spirit. It is no wonder, then, that her writing has received critical acclaim, and that her books have achieved national and international recognition. Many aspiring Chinese American writers have confided that she has been an inspiration and a role model for them.

Maya Ying Lin

A young and gifted architect who has reflected great credit upon Chinese Americans is Maya Ying Lin. Born in this country and raised in Athens, Ohio, she was educated at Yale and Harvard. As an undergraduate at Yale University, she decided in 1981 to submit an entry for the design of the Vietnam Veterans Memorial in Washington, D.C. She envisioned two simple walls of polished black granite with only the names of the slain soldiers inscribed as the monument. The judges unanimously selected her design as the winning entry, but the college senior was unprepared for the storm of controversy that followed.

Because Lin's design did not fit many people's notion of a war memorial, veterans and critics assailed it as "an ugly scar," "a black gash of shame and sorrow," a hideous example of monstrous, modernistic architecture. Others raised questions about her patriotism, her youth, and her sex, and even maligned her Chinese American heritage. However, when the Vietnam memorial was completed and dedicated in 1982, the freshness, emotional power, and tranquil beauty of her design silenced all but the most stubborn of her critics. In 1988, Lin accepted an invitation to design a Civil Rights Memorial in Montgomery, Alabama, to commemorate the struggle and sacrifices on behalf of the civil rights movement in the United States. When the memorial was completed in 1989, etched on it were words drawn from the "I Have a Dream" speech by Martin Luther King, Jr., and partly borrowed from the Bible: "[We will not be satisfied] . . . until justice rolls down like waters and righteousness like a mighty stream." It was an eloquent call for society to hold fast to its ideals, a compelling message that Chinese Americans could easily understand and endorse.

Him Mark Lai

If the past is not to be forgotten, if the painful lessons of history are not to be repeated, one must record the history of Chinese Americans. The treatment accorded to different ethnic and racial groups is a litmus test about the reality of the pledge "liberty and justice for all." Him Mark Lai, an engineer in San Francisco, has long maintained a passionate interest in investigating and documenting the Chinese American experience. Despite being a second-generation Chinese, he is fluent in the Chinese language and has been able to study materials hitherto unexplored by other researchers. Consequently, he has helped to open the field of Chinese American history. Glad to share his knowledge, he has nurtured and encouraged researchers in their quest to place Chinese American scholarship on a solid foundation.

Him Mark Lai does not work alone. His colleagues in the Chinese Historical Society of America, such as Philip Choy, Thomas Chinn, and Judy Yung, have all played an important role in furthering the frontiers of knowledge about the Chinese American experience. Learning from this example, other Chinese communities in Hawaii, Los Angeles, and New York have set up similar historical societies. As more information and materials become available, collaborative efforts can occur between historians and artists or writers. Thus, Academy Award nominee Arthur Dong cooperated with Judy Yung to produce the much-praised *Sewing Woman*, the life history of an ordinary yet exceptional Chinese American woman. Dong later used oral histories to produce *Forbidden City, U.S.A.*, a tremendously informative and entertaining documentary about the famous nightclub in San Francisco's Chinatown from the 1930's to the 1960's.

10 Time Line

1784 "Empress of China" is the first American ship to sail to China for trade.

1789 Chinese arrive in Hawaii.

1839 Opium War begins between China and Great Britain.

1848 Gold is discovered in California, attracting Chinese to the West Coast.

1850 Taiping Rebellion causes turmoil in China; Foreign Miners' Tax legislated in California, the first of several versions that affected the Chinese.

1852 Chinese contract laborers start working in Hawaii.

1854 In *People v. Hall*, California Supreme Court rules that Chinese cannot testify against white persons.

1858 California passes measure to discourage Chinese immigration in the state.

1863 Construction of the transcontinental railroad begins; Chinese are eventually recruited to work on the Central Pacific Railroad.

1868 Burlingame Treaty signed between China and the United States allows citizens to immigrate to either country.

1869 Completion of the transcontinental railroad.

1870 Sidewalk and Cubic Air Ordinances passed in San Francisco, heralding other measures designed to harass the Chinese.

1871 Anti-Chinese riot breaks out in Los Angeles.

1875 Page Law bars Chinese prostitutes, contract laborers, and criminals.

1879 California enacts Second California Constitution with provisions to prevent units of government and corporations from hiring Chinese.

1880   California Civil Code prohibits issuance of marriage licenses between white persons and Chinese.

1882   Exclusion Act bars immigration of Chinese laborers for 10 years; other measures in 1888, 1892, and 1902 extend exclusion, until it is made permanent in 1904 and 1924.

1884   Joseph and Mary Tape sue for their daughter to attend a public school in San Francisco and win; in the next year, the school initiates a segregated "Oriental School."

1886   In *Yick Wo v. Hopkins*, the U.S. Supreme Court rules that a San Francisco laundry ordinance is unconstitutional because it is arbitrarily enforced against the Chinese.

1898   In *U.S. v. Wong Kim Ark*, the Supreme Court recognizes the citizenship of a Chinese child born in the U.S. of parents who themselves were ineligible for citizenship.

1900   Organic Act extends U.S. exclusion laws to Hawaii, which had been annexed in 1898.

1905   China boycotts U.S. products, protesting unfair treatment of Chinese by immigration officials.

1910   Angel Island immigration station opens to screen Chinese immigrants; it operates until 1940.

1911   Chinese revolution brings an end to the Ch'ing dynasty.

1924   Immigration Act excludes aliens ineligible for citizenship, which affects the Chinese.

1927   In *Gong Lum v. Rice*, Mississippi Supreme Court rules that Martha Lum must attend a black school rather than a white one.

1937   Japan invades China after seizing Manchuria earlier in 1931.

1941   U.S. declares war on Japan.

1943   Congress repeals Chinese exclusion acts; Chinese are given a quota of 105 per year and granted the right of naturalization.

1945   War Brides Act and later Fiancees Act allow Chinese women to enter the U.S.

1949   People's Republic of China established on mainland China; Republic of China moves to island of Taiwan.

1950 Korean War begins with subsequent Chinese intervention.

1952 McCarran-Walter Act gives quotas to Asia-Pacific triangle nations and grants naturalization rights, too.

1955 U.S. Confession Program permits Chinese to admit illegal entry in exchange for immunity and legal status.

1959 Hawaii becomes 50th state; Hiram Fong is elected to U.S. Senate.

1965 Immigration Act of 1965 gives Eastern Hemisphere a quota of 170,000 per year with no more than 20,000 per country.

1968 Student strike at San Francisco State University and a later one at the University of California, Berkeley, demanding ethnic studies eventually leads to Asian American Studies programs.

1974 *Lau v. Nichols* decided by U.S. Supreme Court; opens the way for bilingual education programs.

1975 End of Vietnam War and Southeast Asian conflict results in influx of refugees.

1979 U.S. establishes diplomatic relations with Beijing.

1986 Congress gives Hong Kong a quota of 5,000 per year.

1990 Congress grants Hong Kong a quota of 10,000 per year, to be increased to 20,000 per year by 1995.

11 Bibliography

Chan, Sucheng. *Asian Americans: An Interpretive History.*
Boston: Twayne, 1991. A comparative approach to Asians in
the U.S., filled with useful facts and keen insights.
_____ . *This Bittersweet Soil: The Chinese in California
Agriculture, 1860-1910.* Berkeley and Los Angeles: University
of California Press, 1986. The best study on the Chinese in
agriculture, carefully documented.
Glick, Clarence E. *Sojourners and Settlers: Chinese Migrants in
Hawaii.* Honolulu: University Press of Hawaii, 1975.
Adaptation of the Chinese to Hawaii since their arrival in
1789; nicely traced.
Lai, Him Mark; Joe Huang; and Don Wong, eds. *The Chinese of
America, 1785-1980.* San Francisco: Chinese Culture
Foundation, 1980. Fine photographs and interesting narrative,
suitable for young readers.
Lai, Him Mark; Genny Lim; and Judy Yung, eds. *Island: Poetry
and History of Chinese Immigrants on Angel Island,
1910-1940.* San Francisco: Hoc Doi, 1980. Description and
photos of the immigration station and translations of the poetry
left by the immigrants; accessible to young students.
Lum, Arlene, ed. *Sailing for the Sun: the Chinese in Hawaii,
1789-1989* Honolulu: Center for Chinese Studies, University of
Hawaii, 1988. A colorful description of the Chinese
experience in Hawaii; sure to engage young readers.
McCunn, Ruth Lum. *Chinese American Portraits: Personal
Histories, 1828-1988.* San Francisco: Chronicle Books, 1988.
Attractive way to personalize Chinese American history for
young students.

Mark, Diane Mei Lin; Ginger Chih. *A Place Called Chinese America*. Dubuque, IA: Kendall/Hunt, 1982. A highly readable narrative history of Chinese Americans, complemented by photographs.

Nee, Victor G.; Brett de Bary Nee. *Longtime Californ': A Documentary Study of an American Chinatown*. New York: Pantheon Books, 1973. Oral interviews skillfully used; illuminating insights for young students about the different people in a community.

Takaki, Ronald. *Strangers from a Different Shore: A History of Asian Americans*. Boston: Little, Brown, 1989. Moving account with generous use of literature and poetry.

Tom, K. S. *Echoes from Old China: Life, Legends, and Lore of the Middle Kingdom*. Honolulu: Chinese History Center, 1989. A convenient guide to the customs and folklore among Chinese Americans.

Tsai, Shih-shan Henry. *The Chinese Experience in America*. Bloomington: Indiana University Press, 1986. An informed survey of Chinese American history.

Yung, Judy. *Chinese Women of America: A Pictorial History*. Seattle: University of Washington Press, 1986. Useful overview of the diverse experiences of Chinese American women.

Literature and Autobiography

Kingston, Maxine Hong. *China Men*. New York: Ballantine Books, 1980. Rich account of the Chinese American experience brought to life by an extremely gifted writer.

_____ . *The Woman Warrior: Memoirs of a Childhood among Ghosts*. New York: Knopf, 1976. A powerful book that takes the reader on a marvelous journey.

Lowe, Pardee. *Father and Glorious Descendant*. Boston: Little, Brown, 1943. Youth wrestling with identity and acculturation in the period before World War II; interesting for adolescent readers.

Lum, Wing Tek. *Expounding the Doubtful Points*. Honolulu: Bamboo Ridge Press, 1987. Exquisite poems about the poignant and touching moments in everyday life.

Tan, Amy. *The Joy Luck Club*. New York: Putnam, 1989. Heartfelt experiences and commiseration shared among a group of women.

―――――― . *The Kitchen God's Wife*. New York: Putnam, 1991. A mother tells her past to her daughter and reveals an extraordinary story.

Wong, Jade Snow. *Fifth Chinese Daughter*. New York: Harper and Bros., 1950. A second generation girl growing up in San Francisco's Chinatown deals with issues of tradition and change; appealing to young readers.

Yep, Lawrence. *Child of the Owl*. New York: Harper and Row, 1972. A young child must grapple with family problems and develops close ties with her grandmother; enjoyable book for elementary to intermediate level readers.

―――――― . *Dragonwings*. New York: Harper and Row, 1976. An exciting account of a Chinese immigrant who builds a flying machine; a delightful book for young readers.

―――――― . *The Lost Garden*. New York: Messner, 1991. Personal reflections of an award-winning writer of children's literature; mention of crises of growing up as a young Chinese American; helpful for those trying to understand the immigrant heritage.

12 Media Materials

Sources of Information

Gee, Bill J., ed. *Asian American Media Reference Guide*. New York: Asian Cinevision, 1990.

National Asian American Telecommunications Association. *Cross Current Media: Asian American Audiovisual Catalog*. San Francisco:

National Asian American Telecommunications Association, 1990.

Resource Organizations

Asian Cinevision
32 E. Broadway, 4th Floor
New York, NY 10002
(212) 925-8685

National Asian American Telecommunications Association (NAATA)
346 Ninth St., 2nd Floor
San Francisco, CA 94103
(415) 863-0814

Visual Communications
263 S. Los Angeles, No. 307
Los Angeles, CA 90012
(213) 680-4462

Films and Videotapes

"Carved in Silence" (Felicia Lowe Productions, 1987). Felicia Lowe, director. 45 minutes, color. The Chinese American experience at the Angel Island immigration station.

"Chan is Missing" (New Yorker Films, 1982). Wayne Wang, director. 80 minutes, black and white. A mystery that explores the different faces of San Francisco's Chinatown and its people.

"China: Land of My Father" (New Day Films, 1979). Felicia Lowe, director. 28 minutes, color. A Chinese American returns to her roots.

"Chinese Gold: The Chinese in the Monterey Bay" (Chip Taylor Communications, 1987). Geoffrey Dunn, director. 42 minutes, color. History and interviews of Chinese Americans in Monterey.

"Eat a Bowl of Tea" (Columbia Pictures/American Playhouse Theatrical, 1989). Wayne Wang, director. 95 minutes, color. A fascinating look into the bachelor society, based on Louis Chu's novel of the same name.

"Forbidden City, U.S.A." (Deep Focus Productions, 1989). Arthur Dong, director. 95 minutes, color. A documentary about the famous Chinese American nightclub in San Francisco during the 1930's to the 1960's.

"Freckled Rice" (Third World Newsreel, 1983). Stephen C. Ning and Yuet Fung Ho, directors. 48 minutes, color. Experiences of a 13-year-old Chinese American in Boston's Chinatown.

"Mississippi Triangle" (Third World Newsreel, 1983). Christine Choy, director. 110 minutes, color. Examines the 100 years history of the Chinese in the Mississippi delta.

"Misunderstanding China" (CBS, 1972). 52 minutes, color. Somewhat dated, this program was presented as background to Nixon's trip to China. However, it has good footage on American stereotypes about China and Chinese Americans.

"Sewing Woman" (Deep Focus Productions, 1982). 14 minutes, black and white. Arthur Dong, director. A brief but exceptionally satisfying portrait of a sewing woman who exhibits a quiet strength of character.

"Who Killed Vincent Chin?" (Film Makers' Library, 1989). Christine Choy, Renee Tajima, directors. 87 minutes, color. An examination of a case of anti-Asian violence in the U.S., the death of Vincent Chin in Detroit in 1982.

13 Resources

China Institute of America
125 East 65th St.
New York, NY 10021
(212) 744-8181
   Primarily providing lectures and information about Chinese culture in America, the institute occasionally treats topics pertaining to Chinese Americans.

Chinese American Citizens Alliance (CACA)
1044 Stockton St.
San Francisco, CA 94108
(415) 982-4618
   Founded in 1895, this organization tries to advance the concerns of Chinese Americans through participation in politics.

Chinese Culture Center (CCC)
750 Kearny St., 3rd Floor
San Francisco, CA 94108
(415) 986-1822
   Established in 1973, the center is the hub of many activities and exhibits to educate the public about Chinese culture and Chinese Americans.

Chinese for Affirmative Action (CAA)
17 Walter U. Lum Place
San Francisco, CA 94108
(415) 982-0801

An advocacy group, based in San Francisco, serving Chinese Americans.

Chinese Historical Society of America (CHSA)
650 Commercial St.
San Francisco, CA 94111
(415) 391-1188
First organized in 1963, the society has a bulletin, lectures, and an annual journal, *Chinese America*. It also maintains a museum.

Chinese Historical Society of Southern California
P.O. Box 862647
Los Angeles, CA 90086-2647
The society was formed in 1975 and offers lectures and a publication, the *Gum Saan Journal*.

East Wind Books
1435 A Stockton St.
San Francisco, CA 94133
(415) 781-3331, 772-5899
A good source of books about Chinese Americans and Asian Americans, it also offers children's books and Chinese language materials.

Hawaii Chinese History Center (HCHC)
111 N. King St., Rm. 410
Honolulu, HI 96817
(808) 521-5948
Since its incorporation in 1971, the center maintains an active book publications program and issues a newsletter.

JACP, Inc.
234 Main Street
P. O. Box 1587
San Mateo, CA 94401
(415) 343-9408

A non-profit educational corporation founded in 1969, it maintains a wide array of Asian American educational materials. A free catalog is available upon request.

New York Chinatown History Project (NYCHP)
70 Mulberry St., 2nd Floor
New York, NY 10013
(212) 619-4785
Started in 1980, the project gathers historical information and sponsors exhibits and other activities. It also publishes a newsletter, *Bu Gao Ban*.

Organization of Chinese Americans (OCA)
2025 Eye St., NW, No. 926
Washington, DC 20006
(202) 223-5500
A civil rights organization for Chinese Americans, it operates a national office in Washington, D.C. and publishes a newsletter, *Image*.

Wing Luke Asian Museum
407 7th Ave. S.
Seattle, WA 98104
(206) 623-5124
Museum has exhibits pertaining to the Asian American experience with accompanying activities.

INDEX